Topography

Topography

A Pastor's Reflection on the Terrain Between Sundays

Steve Krogh

WESTBOW
PRESS®
A DIVISION OF THOMAS NELSON
& ZONDERVAN

This book is a work of non-fiction. Unless otherwise noted, the author and the publisher make no explicit guarantees as to the accuracy of the information contained in this book and in some cases, names of people and places have been altered to protect their privacy.

WestBow Press books may be ordered through booksellers or by contacting:

WestBow Press
A Division of Thomas Nelson & Zondervan
1663 Liberty Drive
Bloomington, IN 47403
www.westbowpress.com
1 (866) 928-1240

Because of the dynamic nature of the Internet, any web addresses or links contained in this book may have changed since publication and may no longer be valid. The views expressed in this work are solely those of the author and do not necessarily reflect the views of the publisher, and the publisher hereby disclaims any responsibility for them.

Any people depicted in stock imagery provided by Getty Images are models, and such images are being used for illustrative purposes only. Certain stock imagery © Getty Images.

Scripture quotations are from the ESV® Bible (The Holy Bible, English Standard Version®), copyright © 2001 by Crossway, a publishing ministry of Good News Publishers. Used by permission. All rights reserved.

Scripture quotations taken from the New American Standard Bible® (NASB), Copyright © 1960, 1962, 1963, 1968, 1971, 1972, 1973, 1975, 1977, 1995 by The Lockman Foundation Used by permission. www.Lockman.org

ISBN: 978-1-9736-8047-5 (sc)
ISBN: 978-1-9736-8046-8 (e)

Print information available on the last page.

WestBow Press rev. date: 12/20/2019

For a husband and father who is, through and through, a pastor
October 31, 2018

Foreword

There were five specific reasons I fell in love with a Bible/Humanities major at Biola forty years ago. He could make me laugh: he was funny, witty, and clever with words. He was wise, practical, insightful, and always seemed to figure out the right thing to do. He was steadfast in life, constant in temperament, loyal to friends, and dedicated to his studies. He valued family and traditions. He revered God and His word above all else.

Through the years I have seen His Savior faithfully mature and refine him. He has developed a gentleness toward suffering people, an appreciation of the gifts of others, and a deeper dependence on God. Loving God supremely and loving people sacrificially, along with a dedication to the authority of God's Word, has led him to invest almost thirty years as a shepherd of God's church and, for the last four years, in teaching pastors internationally who do not have access to theological education.

As we both approach our sixtieth birthdays, Steve still can make me laugh. I laughed out loud many times while typing into the computer the reflections you will read. He is the wisest person I have ever met. He can work on multiple tasks at the same time, smiling while he does. He figured out how to live well within his means and be generous to many. His steadfastness of character and winsome Gospel-truth analogies have been a ballast for me through six children, four moves, menopause, empty nesting, tragedy and triumphs. Steve is God's gift to me. I am thrilled to gift him today with this collection of his writings.

Lois Krogh
West Chicago, IL
Fall 2018

Preface

Pastor's kid. The perks and pitfalls are well known by all six of us kids. Unrestricted access to the church's dessert freezer and compulsory attendance of youth group weeknight events served as the backdrop to our most formative years. Being a pastor's kid is a defining feature for each of us. We are marked by the rhythms and realities of church life. By God's grace, we are all choosing to continue to live our lives built on church cadences.

God's grace as evidenced through the faithful predictability of our preacher Dad. The Dad that preached sermons in a suit and tie was the same dad that winsomely dialed the phone to order Pizza Hut on a Sunday night (despite mom's reminders that we still had leftovers in the fridge). Dad is the heart of a pastor...he wants to see his people believing and walking in the truth. We really do feel like we, his family, got to be his "first church." Perhaps the place Dad most fully revealed his personality was in his musings on the back page of the church newsletter. Within these articles, the significance of the pastoral role and the intimacy of his role as father often met to reveal the witty and sentimental side of him we all know and love.

These back page articles represent a journey tied to specific location and events. His thoughts were never abstract but deeply tied to place and patterns. Summer backpacks, fall yard work, winter basketball, and spring cleaning projects. His words express the topographic map of our lives.

Reading these articles over a decade later, it's striking how intentional Dad was. He was someone who planned things and did things rather than tell us about the "why" behind them. Without being totally aware of what was going on, we were shaped by the way our dad thoughtfully oriented every aspect of our family life toward Gospel principles.

Dad is someone to be relied on for noticing the significance of a moment, reminding us all that he's seen the cycle of things before, or for concluding "that's just not right" with simple clarity. His lens is astute and poetic, he excels at observation and interpretation. To those who know him as a pastor, these letters are a reminder of his faithful dedication to noticing Gospel truth in every sphere of his life. To his kids, these essays bring us back to the beginning years of our family. We are rooted in the moments and insights outlined in these letters. To us, these collected articles are a reminder of our early years as a family and a testament to how being "the pastor's family" shaped us all. Thank you, Dad.

"For God is not unjust so as to overlook your work and the love that you have shown for His name in serving the saints as you still do." Hebrews 6:10

Derek, Kate & Ted, Kyle & Abby, Jacob, Susie and Luke
San Diego, CA
Waco, TX
San Clemente, CA
West Chicago, IL
Panajachel, Guatemala
West Chicago, IL
Fall 2018

Introduction

The articles that follow are a curated collection of
the "back-page articles" written by Steve Krogh for the monthly
church newsletter while he pastored at Grace Community Church in
Hudsonville, Michigan. In these articles, written over thirteen years,
Steve explores the eternal significance found in temporal places,
everywhere from Niagara Falls to the Krogh family home.

Steve never expected his contributions to church newsletters
to be published. These articles have been collected by his family
in celebration of this 60th birthday. As Steve continues to faithfully
follow the One who charted his topographic map, our hope is that
this book serves as a reminder of the grace of God poured out upon
him and through him. May God continue to use Steve's pastoral
reflections on the terrain between Sundays to delight and edify the
body of Christ.

Contents

2001

Niagara..1
Never the Same..3
A Christmas Reflection..6

2002

February - A Good Month to be Thankful 8
Thoughts on War and Terrorism..10
"What did you think about on Vacation?"..13
Thoughts on Leaf Raking 16
Thoughts on Closing the Pages of Luke's Gospel 19

2003

Things That Matter..21
Reflections on Anticipating Vacation 24
For Everything There is a Season..27

2004

Dads, Daughters and the Sanctity of Life Remembrance..............30
And Another Thing..33
Have you Resolved in the Spirit?..35
The Third Conversion 37

2005

When God Says, "No." 39
Shall We Keep the Traditions Alive? 42

2006

Tugging at Your Heart (and Harp) Strings..................................45

2007

"Got Thorns?" 49
Summer Planning Midwest Style..51
"Raise Your Right Hand but Don't Let Go of That Balloon." 54

2008

"Need a Vacation?"..57
Ten Year Reflections 60

2009

"His Eye is Always Watching. His Hand is Always Moving." 62
The Worry Wart's Prayer...65
"Can You Repeat That?"..68
Three Things I Learned on Vacation..71
"Much Obliged, Lord" 74

2010

The Land of The Red Dust...77
March Madness and Eternal Gladness 81
Pay Your Taxes. . .Honor the Emperor . . . Fear God 85
"Who Gives This Woman?" (Part One) 89
"Who Gives This Woman?" (Part Two) 93

2011

"Do You Believe This?" 98

Speaking Like Christ 101

Marginal Coffee, Good Pastries, Great Book: Lessons from
Bonhoeffer 104

The Danger of Assuming the Gospel: The Lesson of Les Mis 107

Blindness and Tough Love.. 110

King for a Day 113

Thankfulness: God's Will for Luke's Life and Yours....................116

What Has God Given You? 119

Oh, My Aching Back 122

2012

"I Do" - Then Doing It..126

2013

"Sleep Well, My Friend"..129

Feeling Your Pain: A Son's Dislocated Shoulder 132

"You Want to Do What?" 135

Tree of Shame 138

Reflections of a Childhood Home................................... 141

2018

The Tree Line...144

On this your 60th Birthday . . . Letters from Friends.................148

Essays by Themes

Christian Life

Goals and Aspirations (*Have You Resolved in the Spirit?, 2004*)

Money (*The Third Conversion, 2004*)

Our True Citizenship (*Raise Your Right Hand, But Don't Let Go of That Balloon, 2007*)

Worry (*The Worry Wart's Prayer, 2009*)

Living Well in the Seasons of Life (*The Land of the Red Dust, 2010*)

Civil Disobedience (*Pay Your Taxes...Honor the Emperor...Fear God, 2010*)

Believing in the Resurrected Christ (*Do You Believe This?, 2010*)

Our Christ-Like Conversations (*Speaking Like Christ, 2011*)

Accepting Where God has Placed You (*King for a Day, 2011*)

Pain (*Oh, My Aching Back, 2011*)

Sleep and Rest (*"Sleep Well, My Friend", 2013*)

Endurance and Obedience (*Feeling Your Pain: A Son's Dislocated Shoulder, 2013*)

Accepting and Listening to People who Are Different (*You Want to Do What?", 2013*)

Dealing with the Devil and Wrongdoers (*Tree of Shame, 2013*)

Grafted into Christ (*The Tree Line, 2018*)

Christmas

Christ: The Incarnate Servant Serves Through Eternity (*A Christmas Reflection, 2001*)

Importance of Christmas Traditions (*Shall We Keep the Traditions Alive?, 2005*)

Church

Unity and Care for Others (*Oh, My Aching Back, 2011*)

Evangelism

Violinist Joshua Bell and the Beauty of Jesus Christ (*And Another Thing, 2004*)

The Danger of Assuming the Gospel (*The Lessons of Les Mis, 2011*)

Heaven

Anticipating Heaven (*Reflections on Anticipating Vacation, 2003*)

Heaven's "Summer" Never Ends (*Summer Planning Midwest Style, 2007*)

Jesus Christ

Incarnation (*Marginal Coffee, Good Pastries, Great Book, 2011*)

The Risen and Ascended Christ Serves Us (*A Christmas Reflection, 2001*)

The Love of Jesus (*Thoughts on Closing the Pages of Luke's Gospel, 2002*)

The Beauty of Jesus (*And Another Thing, 2004*)

Caeserea Philippi: Even Jesus Took a Vacation (*Need a Vacation?, 2008*)

Judgement Seat of Christ (*March Madness and Eternal Gladness, 2010*)

Believing in the Resurrected Christ (*Do You Believe This?, 2010*)

Our Christ-Like Conversations (*Speaking Like Christ, 2011*)

Essence of Christianity: Jesus (*Marginal Coffee, Good Pastries, Great Book, 2011*)

Full of Grace and Truth (*King for a Day*, 2011)

The Pain of Crucifixion (*Feeling Your Pain: A Son's Dislocated Shoulder, 2013*)

Grafted into Christ (*The Tree Line, 2018*)

Marriage and Parenting

Leaving Your Children a Love for God and Keeping Your Wife (*Things That Matter, 2003*)

Sanctity of Human Life (*Dads, Daughters and the Sanctity of Human Life, 2004*)

Importance of Family Traditions (*Shall We Keep the Traditions Alive?, 2005*)

Family Transitions (*Ten Year Reflections, 2008*)

Crazy Husbands (*Can You Repeat That?, 2009*)

Imperfect Dads, Caring for Mothers, and Contentment (*Three Things I Learned on Vacation, 2009*)

When Someone Wants to Marry Your Daughter (*Who Gives This Woman? Part One, 2010*)

Advice for Dads and Daughters Soon To Be Married (*Who Gives This Woman? Part Two, 2010*)

Parenting Requires Tough Love (*Blindness and Tough Love, 2011*)

Raising Thankful Kids (*Thankfulness: God's Will for Luke's Life and Yours, 2011*)

Keeping Your Vows (*"I Do" - Then Doing It, 2012*)

Flexing on Secondary Things, Respecting Primary Things (*"You Want to Do What?", 2013*)

Don't Be Afraid to Disappoint Your Kids (*"Reflections of a Childhood Home, 2013*)

Missions

Healing of the Nations (*Raise Your Right Hand, But Don't Let Go of That Balloon, 2007*)

National Calamity

God's Sovereignty (*Never the Same, 2001*)

C. S. Lewis on War and Terrorism (*Thoughts on War and Terrorism, 2002*)

Abortion and the Sanctity of Human Life (*Dads, Daughters and the Sanctity of Human Life, 2004*)

Prayer

Joni EarecksonTada: God's Greater "Yes" Above His "No" (*When God Says, "No", 2005*)

Seasons of Life
All Seasons

Living for the Glory of God in Your Season (*For Everything There is a Season, 2003*)

Dry Seasons and Rainy Seasons (*The Land of the Red Dust, 2010*)

Spring

Lessons from Basketball (*March Madness and Eternal Gladness, 2010*)Tax Season (*Pay Your Taxes...Honor the Emperor...Fear God, 2010*)

Summer

Thoughts on Summer Vacation (*What Did You Think About on Vacation?, 2002*)

Anticipation (*Reflections on Anticipating Vacation, 2003*)

Worrying that Summer Goes to Fast (*Summer Planning Midwest Style, 2007*)

Caeserea Philippi: Even Jesus Took a Vacation *(Need a Vacation?, 2008*)

Fall

The Expulsive Power of a New Affection (*Thoughts on Leaf Raking, 2002*)

Winter

Giving Thanks in Winter (*February - A Good Month to be Thankful, 2002*)

The Love of Christ (*Thoughts on the Closing the Pages of Luke's Gospel. 2002*)

Thankfulness

Giving Thanks in Winter (*February - A Good Month to be Thankful, 2002*)

Giving Thanks in All Things (*Much Obliged, Lord, 2009*)

A List of Thanksgiving (*Thankfulness: God's Will for Luke's Life and Yours, 2011*)

Thanksgiving for Salvation, Providence, Sanctifying Trials (*What Has God Given You?, 2011*)

Raising Thankful Kids (*Thankfulness: God's Will for Luke's Life and Yours, 2011*)

Keeping Your Vows (*"I Do" - Then Doing It, 2012*)

Flexing on Secondary Things, Respecting Primary Things (*"You Want to Do What?", 2013*)

Don't Be Afraid to Disappoint Your Kids (*"Reflections of a Childhood Home, 2013*)

Theological Topics

Devil (*Tree of Shame, 2013*)

Gospel: The Danger of Assuming the Gospel (*The Lesson of Les Mis, 2011*)

Grace: Unending, Future Grace (*Niagara, 2001*)

Must Not be Disconnected from Repentance (*Marginal Coffee, Good Pastries, Great ... 2011*)

Makes Blind Eyes See (*Blindness and Tough Love, 2011*)

Grafted into Christ (*The Tree Line, 2018*)

Incarnation: Living With Christians (*Marginal Coffee, Good Pastries, Great Book, 2011*)

Judgement Seat of Christ (*March Madness and Eternal Gladness, 2010*)

Providence: Defined (*His Eye is Always Watching. His Hand is Always Moving, 2009*)

Thanking God For (*What Has God Given You?, 2011*)

Sanctification: The Expulsive Power of a New Affection (*Thoughts on Leaf Raking, 2002*)

Turns to Glorification (*Tugging at Your Heart [and Harp] Strings, 2006*)

Immediate Gratification v. Weeding Out Remaining Sin (*Reflections of a ..., 2013*)

Sovereignty: Should Not Lead to Complacency (*Never the Same, 2001*)

Niagara

When our family stood at the edge of Niagara Falls for the first time, it was quite an impressive sight. I tried to think of something profound to say, but my first thought was similar to what Abraham Lincoln said, when asked what he thought of the great Niagara Falls: "Where in the world did all that water come from?"

I have yet to learn where all that water comes from, but I did learn a few meaningful facts about the Falls. For example, an artist once submitted a painting of Niagara Falls to an exhibition, but neglected to give it a title. The gallery, faced with the need to supply one, came up with this, "More to Follow."

"More to Follow"—an apt name for the Falls that has spilled over billions of gallons per year for centuries.

It is also a fitting emblem to describe the floods of God's grace—always more to follow! The apostle John states, *"For of his fullness we have all received, grace upon grace" (John 1:16),* literally "grace instead of grace" or as others have rendered it, "grace following grace" or "grace heaped upon grace."

Has God been gracious to you? Has He given you what you don't deserve? Has He been good to you? How has He "heaped grace upon grace" to you? The list is inexhaustible: the grace of salvation, the grace of forgiveness, the grace of life, the grace of loving family and friends, the grace of food to eat, the grace of seeing and hearing, of beauty,of music, of color, of future hope. . . .

Perhaps you're anxious about the future. What will happen in this difficult situation? How will this problem be resolved? Will God supply for this particular need? What are you to do with so many unknowns and uncertainties?

Pause for a moment and realize that the same God who has brought you thus far will be with you in the days ahead. His grace that "has brought you safe thus far" will also "lead you home." There is more grace to follow!

In fact, the very purpose of God saving us is to "show in the coming ages the immeasurable riches of His grace in kindness toward us in Christ Jesus." There will be a "Niagara Falls" of God's grace for all eternity, lavished upon believers, so that His full glory may be displayed.

Let us walk today in trust of His future grace for our own lives, our families and our churches.

Never the Same

"Our nation will never be the same." How often did you hear this after the events of September 11? With armed guardsmen at our airport, Coast Guard vessels actually guarding our coastline and American flags flying from many homes and cars, we have tangible evidence that indeed our nation has changed.

Let me ask a more personal question: how has your life changed since September 11? Are you the same person? I trust that my life is different, and I hope yours is too. Let me explain.

Some say that as Christians we are not to be shaken by world events. We have a hope which goes beyond the grave—a hope which the world, the media, and the secular leaders of this day don't understand. We grieve, "but not as those without hope." I agree. God is our refuge and strength, a very present help in trouble. *"Therefore we will not fear though the earth should change,though the mountains shake in the heart of the sea. . .the nations rage, the kingdoms totter, . . .the LORD of hosts is with us; the God of Jacob is our refuge" (Psalm 46:1,2,6,7).*

But, if we are honest, I think many of us had grown a bit too comfortable in the most powerful nation on earth, seemingly invincible to foreign attack.

Likewise, I think it's fair to say that in a church which rightfully and joyfully sings the lyrics:

O Father, You are sovereign
In all affairs of man;
No powers of death or darkness
Can thwart Your perfect plan.
All chance and change transcending,
Supreme in time and space,
You hold your trusting children
Secure in Your embrace.

Sometimes our right comfort in God's sovereignty can grow into a wrong complacency when it comes to the eternal souls of those around us. Ask yourself: has a "God will do what God will do" attitude crept into your heart regarding the salvation of coworkers, family, friends, children? When was the last time you seized a God-given opportunity to direct someone to believe in Christ?

A father in our church shared with me that the events surrounding 9/11 jolted him to realize he has no guarantees regarding how many years he or his children have in this life. He sensed his son's concern as the events were replayed and potential threats set forth on television. This led to a father-son chat about life and death. Eternity. Forgiveness of sin. Right standing before God. All of this culminated in the young boy asking God to forgive his sin as he placed his trust in Christ.

Tears came to my eyes. Not only tears of joy over God drawing someone to Himself, but also tears from a fresh realization that there needs to be a greater urgency in my life to direct others to be reconciled with God. Everyone's time is limited. Everyone's days are numbered.

May God help our heart urgency to be that of the Apostle Paul's: *"Brethren, my heart's desire and prayer to God for them is that they may be saved" (Romans 10:1).*

This Lord's Day, November 11, marks the two-month anniversary of the September 11 events in our nation. Our nation is changed. I trust you are too.

And may we also sing:

We are God's people, the chosen of the Lord,

Born of His Spirit, established by His Word . . .

O let us share each joy and care,

And live with a zeal that pleases Heaven.

A Christmas Reflection

December 2001

Quick, what is the first thing that comes to mind when you think of Jesus Christ in heaven? Before you read on, pause to think. Christ in heaven. Enter heaven—what do you see? How does the risen Savior appear?

Is He clothed in power and majesty? Are angels before Him all veiling their sight? Are saints casting down their golden crowns? Are we joining with the four heavenly creatures to sing "Holy, holy, holy is the Lord God Almighty, who was and is and is to come"?

Yes, those things really will happen. In space and in real time. Those who are followers of Christ will see, hear and experience these things.

But we will also experience something else. This past week as I reflected on Luke's gospel, the following verse leapt off the page at me:

"Blessed are those servants whom the master finds awake when he comes. Truly, I say to you, he will dress himself for service and have them recline at table, and he will come and serve them" (Luke 12:38)

Think about that for a moment. What is Christ doing in heaven? He rolls up His sleeves, pulls out the chair, offers us a seat, and then begins filling cups with water and bringing plates of food—for us!

When Jesus announced, "I am among you as one who serves." (Luke 22:27), He was referring not only to His incarnation and His earthly ministry, but also to eternity, where He serves us!

Until this week, I don't know if I had a category for this. Christ in heaven, the object of our praise? Yes. The Savior is worthy of our worship? Certainly. The One before whom creation bows? Magnificent! I can't wait! But, the servant who will gird Himself with the towel of humility and seat us at the banqueting table of the Marriage Supper of the Lamb? This can't be, but it is!

Why would Jesus do that in heaven for us? I get why He became a servant to wash the disciples' feet, showing them they needed to be cleansed from sin. I can see why He took the form of a servant, laying aside the glory that was rightly His to become an incarnate Savior on earth for those three decades. But, why would He continue in heaven to serve those whom are now redeemed, but also glorified?

Christ seats us at the heavenly banqueting table and serves us so that we will find our joy and delight in the triune God! He serves us so we will fully "taste and see that the Lord is good."

This Christmas season, reflect on Christ in eternity dressed to serve and seat you. The babe in the manger, the Incarnation, is just the beginning. He is "among us as one who serves," not only in Bethlehem's courtyard, but also in heaven's courtyard.

February - A Good Month to be Thankful

February 2002

We've enjoyed a wonderful respite from winter in recent weeks, but the snow is falling again and I'm wondering if it will ever be over. That's why February is a good month to fill our minds with the many benefits God has brought us.

For what it is worth, here are some of things, both sublime and simple, eternal and earthly, serious and not-so-serious that fill my soul with thanks to our great God.

Hager Park provides a quiet place to walk, think and pray through the seasons—moonlit snow in winter, emerging life in spring, morning coolness in the summer and crip leaves underfoot in the fall.

Music that stirs my soul and helps me express truthful praise to God. Isn't it a joy to sing each week with God's people, as well as have others "speak to us in psalms, hymns and spiritual songs"?

The mercy and patience of God, who saved us when we could not save ourselves, and tells us in His Word who did what in salvation and then patiently waits for our response to this to turn from surprise to humility to eager service and reverential worship.

Six children with different personalities, interests and outlooks on life, each of whom as they grow are able to do things I never could (run the basketball court quickly, play the piano skillfully. . . .)

Gemmen's. It's nice to have people who can explain how to fix/repair/replace whatever is broken/missing/in backwards, find it for you on the shelf, and do it without making the mechanically impaired feel subhuman—a real bonus!

And since space is limited, other matters for thanksgiving with no commentary:

- Many friends who ask, "So how are you doing?" And listen to your reply.
- Pastor friends who are in it for the long haul and embrace the joys and sorrows of ministry given from the hand of a sovereign and good God.
- The music of Judy Rogers.
- New books that give a crisp crack when you open them for the first time.
- Old books that have the fountain pen signature of a previous owner.
- Leaves don't fall twelve months of the year.
- People who aren't afraid to get misty-eyed over the right things.
- Elders who think it's a good meeting when all we did was pray.
- People who say, "I'll take care of that for you. Don't worry about it."
- Leather-bound Bibles.
- The hues and shades and colors of creation.
- That God is God and we are not.

Thoughts on War and Terrorism

July 2002

The Bible is a wartime book. Name a book of the Old Testament that lacks connection with war, international upheaval or acts of terror? Hard to do, isn't it? Think of a common Bible story we know well. If you step back and consider the larger picture, it likely is connected with war and international conflict in some way indirectly or directly.

Most of the New Testament was written against the backdrop of looming conflict with the military superpower of the day. Many (if not most) Christians through the history of the church had to live out their faith in perilous times of war and terror.

Thankfully, we have lived free of war on American soil for over half a century. September 11, according to the president, brought "a new kind of war" to our nation. As we create new cabinet positions, prepare stockpiles of vaccines, increase border security and receive frequent "terror alert" bulletins, it begs some subtle questions:

- As a Christian, am I prepared for what may lie ahead?

- Are we, who have lived in relative peace, prepared for times of upheaval other believers have endured for many years?
- How would widespread domestic terrorism or "war brought closer to home" affect my view of God?
- How would it change my life?
- Have I considered biblically what comprises a "just war"?
- Have I prepared my family for times of widespread terrorism and war? Are sons and daughters prepared for what they may experience and be called upon to do?

Author C.S. Lewis enlisted and served as an officer in the Somerset Light Infantry during World War I, reaching the front line in France on his nineteenth birthday, November 29, 1917. After being wounded on Mont Bernanchon during the Battle of Arras, he recuperated and resumed fighting. His roommate and close friend "Paddy" Moore was killed in battle.

During World War II, in the autumn of 1939, Lewis preached a now famous sermon in the Church of St. Mary the Virgin in Oxford, England. In his sermon, "Learning in War Times," Lewis reflected on his own wartime experience and observed, "The war creates no absolutely new situation: it simply aggravates the permanent human situation so that we can no longer ignore it. Human life has always been lived on the edge of a precipice. Human culture has always had to exist under the shadow of something infinitely more important than itself. . . We are mistaken when we compare war with "normal life." Life has never been normal. . . Before I went to the last war I certainly expected that my life in the trenches would, in some mysterious sense, be all war. In fact, I found that the nearer you got to the front line, the less everyone spoke and thought of the allied cause and the progress of the campaign" (*The Weight of Glory*, pg. 44).

Lewis observed that war simply reveals what is in a person's heart, bringing to the surface the real issues of life—the things that really matter.

He closes his sermon by addressing three enemies which war raises up against us: excitement (i.e., war becoming an all-consuming preoccupation distracting us from our God-given tasks), frustration (we can't do the things we had hoped to do) and fear of death and pain.

Perhaps we would all be wise to use this time of relative peace to order our lives so that if the chaos of war and terrorism does come upon us, we may be able by God's grace to continue to glorify Him in all things, as so many of our fellow believers learned to do in times past.

"What did you think about on Vacation?"

This summer, I traveled more than 6,000 miles through fifteen states to return to my roots for a family reunion in San Diego. Here are some of my pastoral musings along the way.

- Pastors always look at church buildings when they drive through towns on vacation.
- If you ask a waitress in the South, "Pardon me, could you repeat that?" and you still don't understand what she said, don't sit there staring at her, just say, "That sounds good, I will have some of that."
- It's embarrassing when it's 105 degrees and your one-year-old cries and screams in that little car on the way to the top of the St. Louis Arch, and people you've never met before are sitting 18 inches across from you in the little cars. Also mumbling, "We really are good parents; really we are" won't convince them.

- You know you are getting a little over sentimental about family bonding on your vacation when you buy a video in the gift shop about the construction of the St. Louis Arch. Maybe it is because you didn't hear the explanation because of your one-year-old's cries.
- Arkansas has more road construction per mile than any state in the union.
- The reason God made Kansas and West Texas is so that kids on driving permits can get in the required hours of driving.
- Texans have more emblems of their state on billboards, signs, clothes and belt buckles than the other forty-nine states combined.
- Texans think that everyone else wants to live in their state.
- It's fun to park on the curb beside the mobile home you lived in when you first got married and tell your kids stories about the newlywed years.
- The students on the seminary campus look younger than you did when a student there twenty years ago.
- Five-year-old daughters get scared in the darkness of Carlsbad Caverns.
- If you're in a hurry, don't plan to get ice cream cones at Whit's End at the Focus on the Family headquarters in Colorado Springs.
- It's great to watch the sunrise from the bottom of Bryce Canyon.
- Your old high school locker combination doesn't work twenty-six years later.
- Your parents will worry about the grandkids jumping off the diving board in their pool the same way they worried about you when you were a kid.

- There are too many people living in California and they drive too fast.
- It's good to laugh with old friends.
- The best memories are usually made doing things that cost the least amount of money.
- The amount of time you spend after your vacation finding Cheerios beneath the car seat is directly proportional to the number of miles you drove.
- Things I like about coming back to West Michigan: the golf courses aren't as crowded as in California. We have the best "Welcome" signs of any state. The beaches have fresh water, the sun sets later in the day, grass is green and people take care of their yards.

I hope you and your family enjoyed the summer, whether you traveled or stayed close to home. I am thankful that God has called me to help shepherd His church, and I am glad that you are a part of our church family. Soli Deo Gloria!

Thoughts on Leaf Raking

October 2002

"Have you ever lived in a home surrounded by trees?" the man who was selling us his home casually asked—after we signed on the dotted line.

"No, but that's one of the reasons we loved your home so much. We think all the trees in the neighborhood are beautiful!" Lois and I replied innocently.

"Well, I hope you enjoy it," he said with a smile.

We forgot all about his question in the excitement of moving to Michigan. What's the big thing with trees? We have trees in California. Two weeks after our autumn arrival, we found out why he was smiling. We also found out why he left us seven rakes in the tool shed.

In our four fall seasons in Michigan, the Krogh family has worn out two of those seven rakes, and has learned a few lessons from the falling leaves. As we prepare for season number five, let me share two thoughts with you.

First, the leaves fall from the trees, not because of death, but because of life. There is new life, new sap flowing through the branches which literally pushes the old leaves off. What looks like present death is actually preparation for future life.

Spiritually, what might look to others (and feel to ourselves) as a "death experience" is actually an experience of life preparing to bud forth. When by God's grace we "put to death what is earthly in you: sexual immorality, impurity, passion, evil desire, and covetousness, anger, wrath, malice, slander and obscene talk" (Col. 3:5,8) it is so that new life may come forth. (Col 3:10). Our spiritual forefathers called this "the expulsive power of a new affection." When God places new love and delights in our lives, it pushes off the "old leaves" of our life.

Perhaps God is calling you to put to death some things in your life. Perhaps you are going through a "death experience." Perhaps there are new delights God is bringing into your life, which are causing former things to be put off.

Second, I have learned that in my fight against the oak leaves, I need a practical plan for their disposal. I have tried a variety of methods with varying success: plastic leaf bags at the curb (once you can no longer see the house it's a little embarrassing), the brown Georgetown Township leaf bags (a bit expensive—will it be saving for the kids' college education this month or buying leaf bags?) or hauling them off under the cover of darkness on a tarp in the back of the minivan? (But then where do I put them and what do I say when the kids ask, "Dad, why are all these crumbled pieces of leaves in my seat?").

Our solution was to build a holding pen behind the tool shed, and then dole out bags of leaves curbside each week through the spring and hope they were all gone before the grass started growing.

Sins, especially those that so easily beset us, don't just disappear magically. We need to have a practical plan for disposing of the deeds of the flesh. Let me offer some plans that I know will work.

"Therefore, confess your sins to one another and pray for one another, that you may be healed. The prayer of a righteous man has great power in its working" (James 5:16).

"Be sober-minded; be watchful. Your adversary the devil prowls around like a roaring lion, seeking someone to devour. Resist him, firm in your faith, knowing that the same kinds of suffering are being experienced by your brotherhood throughout the world" (1 Peter 5:8,9).

"Therefore let anyone who thinks that he stands take heed lest he fall. No temptation has overtaken you that is not common to man. God is faithful, and he will not let you be tempted beyond your ability, but with the temptation he will also provide the way of escape, that you may be able to endure it" (1 Cor. 10:13).

May God give you the expulsive power of a new affection and many seasons of leaf-raking in the years ahead.

Thoughts on Closing the Pages of Luke's Gospel

December 2002

I am not sure what kind of mood the first snowfall of the season puts you in, but I find that it causes me to be reflective—hopefully in a good way. The snow says "slow down. . . take a seat by the living room window. . .watch and listen."

After spending the last two years going through the Gospel of Luke, I have been meditating on these questions: What have I learned and what have I learned about Jesus of Nazareth that I did not realize before? What have I learned about the One whom I will soon meet face-to-face?

I keep coming back to one simple thing: "Behold, how He loved them!" What echoes in my mind is that Jesus truly loved his sheep. He loved those men who hung up their nets in the Galilean sun to follow Him. He loved those women who brought Him warm food and drink. He loved those men gathered in the Upper Room, who followed Him into Gethsemane's olive orchard.

Peter. James. John. Levi. Thomas. He loved Mary, Martha and Lazarus.

He loved a man with a withered hand, a woman with a bent back, a woman wiping his feet with her hair. On and on.

It's easy to think of Jesus as someone who had an important assignment to keep. In fact, His was the assignment of all assignments. After all, He needed to die on the cross for our sin. But now, having walked with Him, listened to Him and watched Him these past months through the pages of Luke's gospel, I see Jesus not only as the great redeemer, but also as the great lover of His people. He doesn't just put up with Peter and his friends. He doesn't just redeem them in obedience to the Father—He actually loves them.

When by God's grace, you sit opposite Jesus at the great banqueting table of the Marriage Supper of the Lamb, what will you think? What will you experience? What will the look in His eyes say to you? Certainly, we will know even more deeply than we do now what it means that He died for us, that He saved us. But, most of all, I think we will sense His great love for us.

During the next snowfall, sit by the window and think about this: Jesus of Nazareth loves you. He knows you. Isn't it amazing to think that He could say to you, as He said to His disciples at the Passover meal in the Upper Room, "with great desire I have desired to eat this meal with you!"

Such love brings many things. Security. Calm. Peace. Hope. Patience. Humility.

May you know the love of Christ in these days.

Things That Matter

As a pastor, I enjoy the weekly routine of interacting with God through His Word, learning new things about Him, His purposes and ways, as well as about me. I also enjoy the "non-routine" events in a pastor's routine such as funerals and weddings.

We usually attend such events in order to express our care for the people and families experiencing either the sorrows or joys of life. This is right and proper.

But, there is another reason we should attend funerals and weddings. Not only is our attendance an expression that we care that our lives are connected with others, but also an opportunity to pause amidst the ebb and flow of life to reflect on things that really matter during our brief sojourn. Last week, I sat in the audience for the memorial service of a beloved saint, listening to wise words and God's Word about what it means to live life well. Tomorrow, I will stand before a young couple, watching them vow their love and life to one another. These are sacred moments.

I trust that my following thoughts will not only be constructive "food for thought," but that they may also encourage you to be more

Topography: A Pastor's Reflection on the Terrain Between Sundays   21

than just a passive observer the next time you express your care in remembering a life or observing the exchange of vows. Here are some reflections regarding things that matter:

1. Life consists of the serious and not so serious. There is a time to be sober, but there's also time to be light-hearted. There is a time to mourn and a time to dance. A time to gather stones and a time to throw them in a lake. A time to have a serious talk with your child and a time to sleep in the tent outside in the backyard. Children and grandchildren are more apt to heed sobering words when they come from someone with a cheerful heart.

2. Most treasured memories involve the simple things of life. Advertisers want us to believe otherwise—that meaning and memories involve money and lots of stuff. Not so. Gather any family as they reminisce about Grandpa or Grandma and they will talk about simple things: walking in the woods on a rainy day, a campfire at the beach, savoring each and every strawberry one at a time. God has made this fine world in such a way that earthly joys are available to kings and princes and the common folks of life.

3. He who leaves his children a love for God's Word leaves them a great heritage. Times change. Fashions come and go. Technology happens. What seems normal and natural for us will seem quaint to our grandchildren. But, "though the grass withers and the flower fades, the word of our God will stand forever." (Isaiah 40:8) Let your sons and daughters, your children's children, see you delight, revere, pore over and honor God's precious Word, and you will give them a timeless, great treasure which lasts for generations.

4. To "keep" is noble. When a husband vows to "keep" his wife (and the children they may be given), he is pledging to be a husbandman, a provider, one who meets physical needs. When children come downstairs each morning and open the cupboard for their bowl for cereal, they are receiving a great gift. Someone likely has risen before them or stayed up late the night before, working. Someone is "keeping" them, providing for their needs, taking consideration of them. The one who makes the vow in youthful marriage makes a vow that spans decades and tens of thousands of hours.

All this from a memorial service and a wedding. You not only "halve sorrows" by attending a memorial service or "double joys" listening to others exchange their marriage vows, you also have an opportunity to pause and reflect on things that matter. May those reflections enable you to live a life well-lived.

Reflections on Anticipating Vacation

May 2003

In a matter of hours our family will be off for a week of vacation adventures on the other side of Lake Michigan in Door County, Wisconsin.

We're looking forward to a number of things:

- a relaxing time by the water in the log-style summer home of some dear friends
- enjoying a Door County fish boil (whatever that is)
- attending the annual Blossom Festival
- sleeping in and eating pancakes in our pajamas at 10:30 in the morning
- visiting so many antique shops that our kids groan, "Not another antique store!"
- losing a few golf balls in the Peninsula State Park Park Golf Course
- watching Horatio Hornblower videos and eating Orville Redenbacher's kettle corn

- renting a pontoon boat to explore the shoreline of Green Bay
- enjoying s'mores and cold milk around a campfire at night
- reading aloud as a family *The Hostage* by Nancy Mankins, wife of New Tribes missionary David Mankins
- finding a few golf balls in the woods of Peninsula State Park Golf Course
- sailing back home to Michigan on the U.S.S. Badger (hopefully on smooth waters beneath a blue sky)

Part of the pleasure of going on vacation is the anticipation. The conversation around the dinner table at our home for the past few weeks has been on all the things I just listed, plus some other anticipated enjoyments.

There is one significant thing about this vacation that Lois and I have kept secret from our kids: Grandpa and Grandma Krogh are flying out from San Diego to join us.

We will pick them up en route to Chicago to join us in Wisconsin, travel back home to Michigan with us and spend another week here before flying back to California.

I can hardly wait to see our kids' reaction when we drive up to the entrance of the hotel near Midway Airport and out walks Grandma and Grandpa!

What's the moral of the story? (There always has to be a moral to the pastor's newsletter, doesn't there?)

Part of the Christian faith involves anticipation. As Christians, we have something we are looking forward to. Mainly heaven. Part of what should bring a smile to our faces now is the anticipation of what is in store for us. Shouldn't that be part of what we discuss around the dinner table with one another? Gardens with no weeds. Work but not toil. Joy with no tears. No sickness. Paradise restored.

What parent doesn't know the joy of planning things for our children to enjoy? Have you found that as your life matures you find your greatest joy in bringing joy to others? It is true what Jesus said. *"It is more blessed to give than to receive" (Acts 20:35).*

For Everything There is a Season

There is a woven tapestry to creation and life. Solomon wrote of this with the words:

"A time to be born, and a time to die;

A time to plant, and a time to pluck up what is planted;

A time to break down, and a time to build up;

A time to weep, and a time to laugh;

A time to mourn, and a time to dance;

A time to tear, and a time to sew;

A time to keep silence, and a time to speak" (Ecclesiastes 3).

One characteristic of living life wisely to the glory of God is recognizing which season you have been in for a while and what corresponding season you need and perhaps have needed for a while.

Let me share the season I am currently experiencing. As I write these words, I sit in the forests of Wisconsin, overlooking a shimmering lake. It's 70 degrees and breezes waft through the oaks and pines. All of nature seems to say, "Slow down and enjoy."

True, there are legitimate, necessary, even meaningful and enjoyable responsibilities in life. Equally true are the many difficulties from which we cannot and must not hide. Yes, we do get a jury summons to appear in court for the month of October. Yes, our kids do get ear infections and don't sleep through the night. Yes, extended family and friends visit. Yes, loved ones get sick and need help. Yes, there are soccer games and music practices to get to. Yes, there are seasons when all these things seem to happen all at once.

All the more reason we need to sometimes enjoy a season of "Be still and know that I am God."

Consider Genesis 2:1-3.

Thus the heavens and the earth were completed in all their vast array. By the seventh day God had finished the work he had been doing; so on the seventh day he rested from all his work. Then God blessed the seventh day and made it holy, because on it he rested from all the work of creating that he had done.

Three times we read, "His work which he had done." Once He finished it and twice He rested from it.

There is "a time to finish the work and rest from it." Perhaps you are in the finishing stages, and God is calling you to a time of rest. Perhaps He wants you to schedule a time of rest months from now. Perhaps your time of rest is ending, and He is calling you to labor again for His kingdom.

A sign of wisdom is knowing what season you are in and what season needs to come. I am thankful for these days of rest, to look back on the good that has been done and be at peace. It is preparing me for what will lay ahead.

What season are you in? Are you thanking God for this particular season of your life? Do you sense this is what He has for you now? Do you see it as your opportunity to glorify Him as well as enjoy Him?

Do you see that this season is just that—a season? Soon it will pass, as surely as fall will give way to winter, winter to spring. Are you looking forward with anticipation and eagerness to a new season? Are you doing anything that shows you understand there is a balance to life?

Finally, how would you fill in the blanks?

"There is a time for _____ and a time for _____."

Dads, Daughters and the Sanctity of Life Remembrance

Many thoughts tumble through your mind as you and your daughters walk for more than two hours with thousands of other people, from the Ellipse outside the White House down Constitution Avenue, past the Washington Monument, past the Department of Justice, past the Capitol, to the steps of the Supreme Court. Here are a few of mine.

- The mind-numbingly statistics of more than 45 million abortions (more than the combined population of 17 U.S. states) since Roe v. Wade legalized abortion in 1973.

- As people stare at us from office windows on Constitution Avenue, what are they thinking? Do they see us as holier-than-thou angry protesters with an issue? Or do they see people with broken and repentant hearts mourning over our nation's sin? Do we convey an "us-versus-them" attitude, as if it's all *their* fault? Or do we corporately own our nation's sin as Nehemiah did when he wrote, "We acted wickedly. . . our kings, our princes, our priests, and our fathers have not kept your law. . . we are slaves. . . "? (Nehemiah 9).

- The inability of man's righteous indignation to accomplish spiritual ends. "For the anger of man does not produce the righteousness that God requires" as James 1:20 reminds us.

- If we plan to erase all references to God from our national psyche, there will be a lot of work for people who are skilled at removing engravings from marble and carvings from polish wood. The phrase "In God We Trust" is carved in the paneling behind the Speaker of the House's chair (directly behind the podium where the president gives the State of the Union Address). Scripture references abound in special blocks in the Washington Monument. God's name is often found in stone and wood, as well as on canvas, throughout Washington D.C.

- How would things be different if we lived in a nation that didn't protect its citizens? What if the horse-mounted police cordoning the sidewalks belonged to a repressive regime? Would we still be so bold? Do we really understand what it's like for many of our brothers and sisters in Christ around the world who daily face tribulation for being followers of Christ?

- My daughters carry long stem roses during our walk, a symbol of the preciousness of life and the unique privilege given to women of nurturing and sustaining life. Do my daughters see their dad as someone who honors their mother for the sacrifices she makes daily? Do my words and actions cause my daughters to embrace their femininity and to look to the future with a confident, expectant smile as they find their way in life? (See Proverbs 31:25.)

- Do people in our congregation who have had an abortion or encouraged a woman to have one sense each Lord's Day that there is mercy and forgiveness for them? Do they see level ground at the foot of the cross? Do they see their fellow believers bowing humbly to drink from the same fount of mercy as they? Do all of us arise each week to serve our gracious God with renewed vigor and courage?

As our small group of dads and daughters reaches the steps of the greatest court in our land, we bow to pray and our prayers are heard in the supreme court of the universe. Will He who hears our prayers have mercy on our nation? Will He heal our land? Will we live to see just laws in our land? Will Roe v. Wade be overturned in our day? If so, will we see this as the end of the journey, an argument won or as a gracious new beginning for our nation?

Those are just some of my thoughts as we walk together in our nation's capital. May God have mercy on us!

And Another Thing

Every once in awhile I plan to say something in a Sunday sermon which, for whatever reason, didn't get said—so here is what I planned to say last Sunday.

Do you remember when Joshua Bell, the-$1,000-a-minute concert violinist, posed as an unknown street musician at a Washington D.C. Metro station and played on his $3.2 million Stradivarius? More than a thousand people rushed by in 42 minutes without ever slowing down to listen. A few people did toss some quarters or dollar bills in his open violin case.

However, one YouTube video shows a lady holding a white bag, stopping and listening intently to Joshua Bell. Her name is Stacy Furukawa, and she had recently seen Joshua Bell perform live at a free concert at the Library of Congress. When she heard the music and saw his face, she recognized him and stopped to enjoy the moment. As she stood eight feet away smiling, Joshua Bell knew that he had been recognized, and he began to smile as he continued playing. When he finished playing, they greeted one another.

It is all captivating to watch, but if you look carefully, you will notice that when Stacy Furukawa stopped to listen, others stopped as well. It's as if when Stacy planted herself eight feet from the violinist and listened intently with a smile on her face, it gave courage to others to do the same. It's as if people need someone else to stop and listen before they sense the freedom to do the same.

Watch the person leaning against the pillar. Look at the person standing in the corner. The other person who slows down, turns his head and stops. Stacy standing there, feet planted, gaze set, smile on her face empowers others to stop and listen as well. You can almost hear them thinking, "Well, if she thinks this is worth listening to, maybe I should, too." Or, "If I stop I won't look foolish, because she has already stopped."

Now picture the person at the cubicle next to you or in the same building. Picture the fellow student who sits behind you in class. The neighbor who always waves as you drive past. The friend you golf with. The person you've known since high school.

None of them are Christians as far as you know. The culture tells them, "There is nothing beautiful about Jesus Christ." The devil whispers, "No music to listen to here." Even their own hearts tell them, "Don't stop. Just keep doing what you are doing. You won't find anything there. Move on."

Then they see you and think, "But he stopped," or "Apparently she thinks there is something to listen to. Look at the smiles on their faces. They have found peace, something to treasure and enjoy."

Does your life convery delight in knowing Jesus Christ? Do others sense that you enjoy the music that accompanies a follower of Christ? That there is something to savor and treasure about being His follower?

May you and I so enjoy Christ and the life He brings, that others can't help but stop and listen to His music and find life in Him as well.

Have you Resolved in the Spirit?

May 2004

"Now after these events Paul resolved in the Spirit *to pass through Macedonia and Achaia and to go to Jerusalem, saying, 'After I have been there, I must also see Rome.' And having sent to Macedonia two of his helpers, Timothy and Erastus, he himself stayed in Asia for a while" (Acts 19:21-22).*

If you asked the Apostle Paul, "Do you know exactly what you will be doing six months from now? How about a year from now? Three years?" I think he would say, "Not exactly. But Lord willing, I do have some things God has put on my heart to accomplish for His kingdom. All my hopes and plans are subject to 'if the Lord wills,' but, yes, I have some goals of what I would like to do. May I share them with you?"

This passage in Acts reveal that Paul had both short-term (Macedonia, Achaia, Jerusalem) and long-term goals (Rome) and practical steps to achieve those goals (send Timothy and Erastus ahead to Macedonia on a fact-gathering trip). Goal setting and achieving goals is not a modern American concept, but an ancient, biblical, trans-cultural practice.

The writer of Proverbs tells us, *"The plans of the diligent lead surely to abundance" (Proverbs 21:5)*. Indeed, we could say that it is what human beings do because they are made in the image of God.

Notice that Paul resolved in the Spirit to do certain things. His goals, dreams and aspirations were not self-originating pipe dreams. Paul didn't sit down and say, "Now what would I like to do?" Rather, his aspirations were brought under the direction and refinement of the Holy Spirit. Yes, Paul did resolve to do certain things, but his resolve was "in the Spirit."

How would you complete the sentence: "I have resolved in the Spirit to . . . .?" Do you have aspirations that are submitted to God, which he has refined and purified? Do you have plans and goals you'd like to accomplish for the sake of the kingdom of God? Are you taking practical steps towards those goals?

This summer, spend time thinking, dreaming and praying about short-term and long-term goals for the kingdom of God. Whether you are a young person with your life before you, or raising a family in the middle of life's busyness or watching your nest empty out or enjoying the sunset years of life, God has a purpose for you. Ask God to help you "resolve in the Spirit" for the glory of His kingdom!

The Third Conversion

Several weeks ago, I placed above my computer screen this quote from Martin Luther: "There are three conversions: the conversion of the heart, the mind and the pocketbook."

How does this strike you? Anything seem a bit odd or unusual? Leave it to Luther to pack a punch. He did not say "the conversion of the heart, the mind and the soul." That would be nice and safe. Instead, he startles us with the third conversion: the pocketbook.

Why bring the pocketbook up? I think Luther brings it up because Jesus brought it up. John the Baptist brought it up. The apostle Paul brought it up. All the writers of Scripture bring it up. The Bible's teaching about material possessions is inseparably connected to genuine faith and conversion.

For the overwhelming majority of Christians I know there has been a conversion of the heart. They have come to the realization that their sin separated them from a holy God, and that the reconciliation they needed is found only in Christ and only by trusting in His work upon the cross.

There was the second conversion of the mind when they realized what it truly means that salvation was all of God's grace. He took the initiative, not us. He first loved us. And that loving initiative did not begin when one responded to the gospel. It did not begin when one heard the gospel. It did not even begin when God gave His Son at Calvary. It began before the creation of this galaxy when God chose those to be redeemed! The conversion of the mind is when one sees that God is at the center of the spiritual universe, and that since salvation was all of God's grace, our response to Him of obedience was motivated by grace.

These first two conversions are an ongoing process, not simply a past event. Our hearts and minds continue to grow in love and knowledge of God.

If you were to ask me if these same Christians had a conversion of the pocketbook, I would have to answer, "I'm not sure." Certainly there are some whose pocketbooks bear the marks of radical conversion. They are good stewards and generous givers. They make wise and bold investments in kingdom work. But if we were honest, many of us would admit, "My pocketbook needs converting." I know mine does. Let us ask God to do another grace-endowed conversion in us.

When God Says, "No."

From her wheelchair, Joni Eareckson Tada, surveyed the Pool of Bethesda in Jerusalem, the site of Jesus healing the lame man (John 5), and wrote these closing words in her book, *The God I Love.*

"A flurry of dust swirled at my feet as a warm, dry breeze rose and tossed my hair. I was speechless. Large tears welled in my eyes, and I sniffed hard, as I imagined blind people clustered against the wall, and the lame leaning against the pillars. I could see the paralyzed people lying on stretchers and mats, their eyes searching and their hands pleading. And I saw myself among them, dressed in a burlap cloak, lying on a mat, squeezed somewhere between a shady, cool wall and the paralyzed man who had been there thirty-eight years.

"Another dry breeze touched my wet face. Oh, Lord, you waited more than thirty years to bring me to this place. I gulped hard, remembering the times I'd lain numb and depressed in my hospital bed, hoping and praying that Jesus would heal me, that he would come to my bedside as he did with the man on the straw mat, that he would see me and not pass me by.

"And now after thirty years I'm here. I made it. Jesus didn't pass me by. He didn't overlook me. He came my way and answered my prayer—he said no.

"I turned my thoughts, my words, heavenward. 'Lord, your no answer to physical healing meant yes to a deeper healing—a better one. Your answer has bound me to other believers and taught me so much about myself. It's purged sin from my life, it's strengthened my commitment to you, forced me to depend on your grace. Your wiser, dear answer has stretched my hope, refined my faith, and helped me to know you better. And you are good. You are so good.'"

As our church filled last Friday night to remember the grace of God in Lyle Howard's life, I thought of Joni's words: "Your no answer to physical healing meant yes to a deeper healing—a better one." We spoke, heard, prayed, sang, wept, believed and worshipped Friday night regarding that "better healing."

But consider Joni's next words: "Your (no) answer has bound me to other believers." That, too, has happened. Adversity has brought the body of Christ together. When one suffers, all suffer together.

On more than one occasion in these last weeks, I watched the body of Christ in action at the Howard home. Though a pastor, I was more a silent observer than a vocal participant. I saw brothers and sisters in Christ "bound to one another." I saw people engaged in a battle, zealous for the reputation of God and the good of His child. Being "bound to one another" is costly, yet joyfully precious.

Sometimes "being bound to others" involves a deliberate choice to love and care. Sometimes it is purposeful, intentional. Sometimes it draws a circle and draws another in. Other times we are "bound to others" by the providential circumstances of our sovereign God. God draws the circle for us.

As God binds us to one another, may we see God's greater "yes" behind, about and over His "no."

Shall We Keep the Traditions Alive?

April 2005

Older sister Kate shuddered at the thought of her four-year-old brother, Luke, growing up in a home with, yikes, of all things, an artificial Christmas tree. How low could a family go?

Sensing that I wasn't racked with the appropriate amount of parental guilt, she immediately added, "And what about all the Christmas traditions I grew up with and have such fond memories of? Remember making those ice candles? How we had to find half gallon milk cartons, drink all the milk, fill it with ice cubes and pour in the hot wax? Then after it cooled we would light the candle and watch the colored wax flow through the openings? What will happen to poor Luke if *(sob, sob)* he doesn't grow up with these things?"

Being skilled at Kate's game, I had my ready defense. "Ah, but who is it that leaves the comfort of the warm van to pirouette evergreen trees, one by one, on the icy tree lot on Chicago Drive, silently pleading to the warm faces in the fogged up van, 'How about this one? Does it look good? Will Mom like it? Is there a bare spot I can't see since my face is buried in its wet, prickly needles?'"

Feeling smug, I play my trump card. "Who is it that straps the tree on the roof of the van and prays that the bungee cord won't come off on the corner of Baldwin and Chicago Drive?" Then with the look of glee, I administer the coup de grace, "And just who is it that disposes of the tree in an environmentally acceptable fashion that's preserving the ozone layer for one more year? And speaking of ozone, wouldn't that ever important layer be better off if we did get an artificial tree?"

Humble silence reigns. After such a devastating blizzard of rhetorical questions, one need not even stoop to address such things as lowly as milk carton ice candles.

Or so I thought.

Motivated not by parental guilt, but pastoral reflection, I ponder, "Why do we have traditions? Why did I teach my kids how to make those ice candles just like my father did with me?"

Could it be that in an ever-changing world, where half-gallon milk cartons are increasingly hard to find and technology advances daily, it is important to have a connection with one's roots? That children need to know that we aren't left to figure it all out on our own? That though this month's "latest and greatest" device makes last month's obsolete, some things transcend the generations?

It's comforting for our kids and grandkids to know that "my dad did it this way when he was a kid. One day I will teach this to my kids. Life will work. Things change, but it will be okay."

And there are some things even more comfortable than ice candles and real Christmas trees. Parents spending time with their kids. Like Dad doing what dads do. Like mom being moms. Like loving, caring, listening, laughing, enjoying, creating, remembering.

So as you drive by Chicago Drive one wintry night this week, yes, that will be me doing the "Evergreen Pirouette" one more time. I am not doing it for the eighteen-year-old son or seventeen-year-old daughter. Or even for four-year-old Luke. I am doing it for the generations to come should our Lord's second advent be delayed.

What are your traditions? Are you keeping them alive? And what about passing down to the next generation the greatest tradition of all—a reverence and love for God. May we instruct our children and our children's children as Mary did when she found out that she was to bear the Messiah, "His mercy is for those who fear him from generation to generation." (Luke 1:50).

Tugging at Your Heart (and Harp) Strings

May 2006

We wind our way through the narrow streets of Chicago's West Side, and as the "L" rumbles overhead, we know we are out of our element. Then my daughter shouts, "There it is!" and points to the burgundy awning of the Lyon & Healy Harp factory.

For the next hour, a ten-year old daughter and her forty-year old father watch in awed silence as master craftsmen turn pieces of sitka spruce and tight-grained mahogany into some of the world's most exquisite instruments. We watch with quiet respect as chunks of wood are sawed, turned, glued, clamped, chiseled, painted, lacquered and gilded.

Up three stories we climb in what many regard as the greatest harp factory in the world. I am entranced by a group of workers who are producing something greater than the mere sum of their parts. A symphony is being played and their instruments are lathes, band saws, planer and sanders.

Eight years later we returned to the same factory. This time things are different. My daughter now brings her harp for regulation, a final tune up for a senior recital. The young girl is now a young woman. Things have changed for me as well. The stairs seem a bit longer and steeper.

The factory is different, too. The burgundy awning is still there, but you no longer step through the door and into the showroom. "The showroom has been moved upstairs," I am told. Yes, indeed it has. Now you don't get to see the finished product until the end of the tour, unless you take the express elevator right to the top. Get off on the fourth floor and make a left. You will then be dazzled as well-placed lights cast their spell over sixty of the world's finest harps. Take your pick. Choose your wood and color, size and shape.

What did I learn from this second trip to the factory?

I once heard a preacher say, "This world is just the workroom. The showroom is upstairs." His point? This life is the prelude to something greater. You have to go through the sawing, chiseling, gluing and clamping before you get to the showroom. The sawdust and fumes are all part of the necessary process to get to the showroom floor. As they say, "No pain. No gain."

Though the folks at Lyon & Healy likely don't consider themselves theologians, they got their theology right when they "moved the showroom upstairs." Glorification follows sanctification and not the other way around.

But, I ask, "Is that how we like it?" If we are honest, we sometimes wish the showroom was still on the first floor, right inside the door. Who wants to mess with all the sanding, fitting and re-fitting? Who has the patience for the intricate carving, not to mention the gilding with those fragile flakes of gold? Who wants to wear safety goggles and breathe through a mask? We grow tired of the refining process and want heaven's joy now "I'm tired of being refined," we sigh. Enough already.

"Not interested in the factory tour? Just take the express elevator and push number four. It will take you right to the top," the receptionist intones. That's how a lot of people want their sanctification: take the express elevator and get right to the showroom floor. No bending of wood. Skip all the scraping. No refashioning. No hang time drying. No need to apply a second coat. Take me to the bright lights. Now.

There is only one problem. Perhaps the owner of the factory moved the showroom upstairs for a reason. Maybe He knows what He is doing. We think it would be easier to have the showroom immediately accessible on the ground floor, maybe easier isn't always better in the long run.

There is a final kicker from the theologians at Lyon & Healy. There is more than a showroom now on the fourth floor. I crack open a door and find a beautiful concert hall, with a huge picture window perfectly framing the Chicago skyline.

I pick up a program left on one of the seats—just two nights ago these old brick walls and polished wood floor were graced by the music of one of the harp world's masters. "It was beautiful," our host proudly says. "A great evening."

Here is the point. Sanctification for sanctification's sake would be pointless. All this refining—for what? No, there must be more to life than just the factory. There must be a fourth floor. There must be glory coming. But what is glory? Is it the bright lights and lines of elegant harps, quietly arrayed? Is the glory the showroom where money talks, but the music is not heard? The goal certainly is not just to make instruments, but neither is it just to sell them.

The glory of the fourth floor is the concert hall. The glory of Lyon & Healy is when the instruments are played and enjoyed. The glory is when the strings are plucked, the music is heard, hearts stirred and beauty tasted.

One day, the sanding and scraping will be over. We will lay down our safety glasses and masks. No more chiseling and restringing. We will be ushered upstairs and the music will begin. Our sanctification will turn to glorification . . . . in the concert hall.

On that day we won't just be watching, listening and applauding while others play their instruments. All who are in Christ will sing and play like we never have before.

And the music will never come to an end.

"Got Thorns?"

March 2007

There is a great scene in the *Amazing Grace* movie about William Wilberforce's lifelong quest to abolish slavery in the British Empire more than two hundred years ago. Wilberforce, a member of parliament in his young twenties and his good friend William Pitt, who became prime minister at the tender age of twenty-four, are enjoying some good-natured horseplay on a morning exercise run.

They have been at their responsibilities awhile, and they are no longer naïve to the cost of public service and positions of responsibility.

Since they lived in the days prior to Nike footwear, they are running barefoot. As they finish their run and are walking home, one of them painfully steps on a thorn and says, "Funny, how when you are running, you don't feel the pain of the thorns." Then, referring to the significant tasks before them, he concludes: "Let's keep running!"

Life is the same way, isn't it? When we slow down, get tired, start to give up. . . then we feel the thorns. Perhaps it is the thorn of discouragement. Or the thorn of doubt. Or the thorn of criticism. Or the thorn of fear. When we are running the race, for some reason, we can step on the thorns and keep going.

The writer to the Hebrews says, *"Let us run with endurance the race that is set before us, looking to Jesus, the founder and perfecter of our faith" (Hebrews 12:2).*

As we grow older, our pace will decline a bit. That is natural. Yet sometimes we lose our momentum a bit too soon. We slow down too much and aren't running as we should.

Is there an area in which you need to pick up the pace a bit? Have you slowed down when it comes to serving others with zeal? Spending time in the Word? Keeping up with a friend? Spending time with your spouse? Getting in shape? Keeping your commitments to the church body?

Sometimes when you feel the prick of the thorns, it's just an encouragement to "Keep on running!"

Summer Planning Midwest Style

One of the things that impressed me about West Michiganders when we moved here nine years ago was how well everyone planned their summers. Before the snow was fully melted, everyone knew exactly what they were doing each week of June, July and August. If I asked someone in late February, "What will you be doing on the third Saturday of June? or "How about the last Monday of July?" they could calmly answer, including at no additional cost the added insight, "Did you know there will be five Mondays in July this year?" "Uh, no. I didn't know. Thanks for the tip." "You're welcome. Plan accordingly." Then in a hushed tone, glancing sideways, they whisper, "There was a cancellation at 11:00 p.m. last night on the only remaining site at Hoffmaster State Park for the month of August. If you act quickly, you may be able to get it."

So, what gives?

I think, in part, the answer is found in the all important phrase, "Before the snow was fully melted." In California, summer begins in April and ends well into October, and there is plenty of time to do whatever you desire. No need to rush things. When summer shrinks to eight, maybe ten weeks as it does in Michigan, it's "You snooze, you lose."

A result is that though we may cherish our summer months more than most, we also can get overly anxious about how we spend our limited supply of summer. We can hoard our summer weeks. We can get overly punctilious and wound up pretty tightly over how we plan to relax on vacation. Then we worry that the summer has gone too fast.

The next time you get your calendars out and the conversation sounds similar to ours: "This week is the missions trip. This week is the high school trip to West Virginia. Katie has French in summer school until July 17. Derek's college classes begin August 22. We get back from Cameroon on June 27. That means we have these five days here that we can. . ."

I encourage you to do two things: First, think about the verses I read late last night.

"They will see his face, and his name will be on their foreheads. And night will be no more. They will need no light of lamp or sun, for the Lord God will be their light, and they will reign forever and ever" (Revelation 22:4,5).

There will be no need to worry about eternity's "summer" coming to an end. You will never say, "Wow, it's almost over. Where did the summer go?" The enjoyment of the new heaven and new earth will last forever. And forever is a long time. As C. S. Lewis said, "The joy never ends." That should cause us to take a deep breath, recognize that though our Michigan summers may be short, eternity's pleasures are forever.

Second, perhaps we should look for an opportunity to give away a portion of our summer. Maybe we should look for a way to spend some of our limited and precious days to give rather than receive.

Perhaps you will schedule a few times this summer to have someone over for a barbeque and an evening of good conversation, focusing on caring for others. Perhaps you will organize a block party for your neighborhood and share the love of Christ with others. Perhaps you will spend a quiet day at home this summer and instead of spending money doing this or that, you will give to someone in financial need.

And yes, there are five Mondays in July this year. Plan accordingly.

"Raise Your Right Hand but Don't Let Go of That Balloon."

As the sun streams through the window of the Gerald R. Ford Presidential Museum that overlooks the Grand River on a crisp, blue-skied fall morning, the federal judge reads the names of over thirty countries. Beginning with Afghanistan and ending with Zimbabwe, it is literally a roll call of nations from "A" to "Z".

As the nations are announced, one by one more than eighty people stand. They raise their right hands to renounce former allegiance and pledge their lives to a new country, promising to defend their new homeland from all enemies, both foreign and domestic.

An elderly, wrinkled couple from Vietnam stands near a handsome Italian man in a well-pressed suit (presumably from Italy as well). The bearded, turbaned man from India rises from the same row as the veiled Afghani. The exuberant Iranian leaps to his feet waves to the crowd and gustily proclaims, "I am so proud to be an American!" and nearby the group from Bosnia/Herzegovina rises to their feet in quiet nervousness. The eyes of the tribal-scarred faces from Sudan shine with the same joy as the fair-skinned Romanians.

On this day, the differences no longer matter. Each took a different route from a distant land, but today they raise their right hands as one.

Lois, the kids and I are happy for Emmanuel, our foster son, who now is proudly a citizen of the United States of America. We are so glad that his journey has brought him to this great country. The judge tells him and the others all the good things about America. Our helium balloons proclaim "U.S.A." America's newest citizen celebrates by taking us all out to Bob's Big Boy—what could be more American than that?

But my mind is no longer thinking of red white and blue. What will that day be like when people from not fifty, but every nation gather along the grandest river of all?

> *"Then the angel showed me the river of the water of life, bright as crystal, flowing from the throne of God and of the Lamg through the middle of the street of the city; also, on either side of the river, the tree of life with its twelve kinds of fruit, yielding its fruit each month. The leaves of the tree were from the healing of the nations. They will see his face and his name will be on their foreheads. . . . for the Lord God will be their light, and they will reign forever and ever" (Revelation 22:1-5).*

That day as we lift our hands in praise to our Redeemer, the differences will truly not matter. All the "lost boys" and "lost girls" and "lost men" and "lost women" will be home. Our different routes from distant lands will lead us to a common throne.

Let me close with a few questions. Where is your ultimate, lasting citizenship? "But our citizenship is in heaven, and from it we await a Savior, the Lord Jesus Christ" (Philippians 3:20). Have you raised your right hand in allegiance to Christ? Are you defending His kingdom and church from all enemies foreign and domestic? If so, how? If not, how can you?

Finally, does your faith in Christ impact the "roll call of nations?" Are you sharing Christ with those who have come to this country? Do you have a relationship with a brother or sister in Christ that transcends style of clothes or color of skin or mother language? Do differences matter to you or do you find that a common Savior transcends all these things? Do you pray often for the "healing of the nations?" Who do you know that is living for Christ in a distant land where life is hard? How are you helping them?

> "And the city has no need of sun or moon to shine on it, for the glory of God gives it light, and its lamp is the Lamb. By its light will the nations walk, and the kings of the earth will bring their glory into it. They will bring into it the glory and the honor of the nations" (Revelation 21:23, 24, 26).

"Need a Vacation?"

By popular demand the Krogh family vacationed last week in the Porcupine Mountains in the U.P. We trekked twenty miles, carried our earthly necessities in backpacks, slept on terra firma, doused ourselves with Deet, even wearing mosquito head nets at times. Why such fun? Why was the demand popular?

Several months ago we put it to a vote, and the family overwhelmingly voted to go backpacking because, and I quote, "Luke (the six-year-old) has never been backpacking, and it will be fun to watch him do it." As the week approached, the soon-to-be-fifty-year-old parents began to have second thoughts. "Hey, the two oldest kids who voted for this aren't even going because they have to work. The election was rigged." We went.

The trails seem a bit longer, the uphills a bit steeper and the packs a bit heavier as you get older, but there are joys that make it all worthwhile. Shining Cloud Falls on the Big Carp River is one of the most incredibly beautiful places I have ever camped in my life. There is nothing like watching the sun melt into a calm Lake Superior, as you gather around a campfire on the beach with no one else in sight.

Why do we do this thing called vacation? The dictionary defines it as "a period of time devoted to pleasure, rest or relaxation."

Sometimes it is difficult for people to be off duty and enjoy pleasure, rest and relaxation. Sometimes it is difficult for us, as Christians, too. Somewhere we picked up the idea that pleasure is bad, rest is for when we get to heaven and relaxation is for slackers. Maybe we even think, "Would Jesus go on vacation? Certainly not!"

I remember years ago visiting Caesarea Philippi, where Jesus asked the disciples the famous question, "Who do people say that the Son of Man is?" While others answered John the Baptist, Elijah, Jeremiah, etc., Peter went to the head of the class when he answered, "You are the Christ, the Son of the living God" (Matthew 16:16).

I remember the tour guide informing us, "People came to Caesarea Philippi for only one reason in Jesus' day. Look around you." In the middle of an arid, parched area, we stood knee deep in a beautiful, cool, crystal-clear, spring-fed river. "This is where the Roman armies would come for a little R & R, rest and relaxation," the guide told us.

I smiled as I thought of Jesus taking his little band of soldiers to this beautiful spot. Did He have an important lesson to teach them about His identity? Was it important for them to get their theology right? Was this teaching important to the mission that needed to be accomplished? Yes on all counts. But why did He take them to this beautiful oasis for this lesson rather than ask the question in the middle of the hot desert?

Is it because He knew that they needed "a period of time devoted to pleasure, rest or relaxation?" Is it because He knew that He too needed it? I think so.

I hope your theology tells you that Christ is true deity—truly God, the Christ, the Son of the living God. I hope your theology also tells you that Jesus is true humanity. He felt the cool, sapphire waters run over His hairy legs. He enjoyed the beauty of a spring-fed stream.

Whether your vacation takes you to the Big Carp River with the Shining Cloud Falls or Caesarea Philippi or somewhere in between, I hope you will truly enjoy your time devoted to pleasure, rest and relaxation. May it be a little taste of heaven, and may it cause you to love our Savior more.

Ten Year Reflections

October 2008

Ten years ago, our family made the transition from a rural church in Northern California, where I had pastored for thirteen years, to a suburban church in west Michigan. We left friends, people we loved and the land we knew (granted, the land of "fruits and nuts") to come to unknown "Dutch Territory" (What kind of place would call itself "Michigan's Salad Bowl"?). Here are some reflections on this ten-year anniversary.

The Trek: Lois, Katie, Susie and Jacob (mending from a broken femur) flew out. Derek, Kyle and I made the journey an adventure, pitching our backpack tent along the road for the four or five nights of our cross-country trek. The very first October night, with the wind sweeping across the high desert of Nevada, was all kind of desolate and spooky, so we chickened out and got a hotel. So much for adventure. The backpacks and tent never came out of the car.

The Greeting: After living in a parsonage, it was exciting to think of having our first home. When we arrived, ladies in the church had spent hours cleaning and polishing. One man had put up some molding, some others had painted, one woman had put hay bales and corn stalks in our front yard, new carpeting was in and several had made sure the pantry was stocked with more goodies than should be legal. I remember the kids looking with big eyes at all the packages of Oreos, saying, "I think we are going to like living here!"

Surprises: I wasn't too sure what it meant when the assistant pastor presented us with a leaf rake and a toboggan on our first Sunday morning in October. But, in about two weeks I found out what the rake was for and two months later, well . . . you get the picture.

Storms: Our first winter here, the electricity went out, limbs blew off trees and through the roof of our shed, neighbors were firing up generators. A friend came over and wired a generator through a window into the basement and said, "You get the refrigerator, the bathroom light and one other room. Which one do you want it to be?" I tried to calmly ask, "Does this happen often?" He looked at me somewhat puzzled and said, "At least we don't have earthquakes here."

More Surprises: "Honey, I am going to the doctor today," Lois said. Later that day the forty-two year old parents found out there was going to be a "Michigan baby" to go along with those California kids! I was preaching through the gospel of Luke at the time, so we choose "Luke" for a name. It's good I wasn't preaching through Nahum.

Being a Pastor: I could fill up pages here. Ultimately, the Lord will render his evaluation on all of our lives, all we have done for the Kingdom, all we have done in the vineyard where He sent us. He will have His verdict of this church and our time here. Until then, it brings me great joy to see a body of people who truly are learning what it means to "Love God supremely. Love people sacrificially." It is a joy to serve with others whose heartbeat is the same. It is a joy to hear again and again from visitors that "this is the friendliest church we have ever known!"

"His Eye is Always Watching. His Hand is Always Moving."

I keep being encouraged by the definition of God's providence that our daughter Susie shared with me from her sixth-grade Bible study hour class. "His eye is always watching. His hand is always moving."

Think of that. God's eye is always watching because He never sleeps or grows drowsy. He never loses interest and nods off. He never takes a day off. He never goes on vacation. He is always watching because nothing can be hidden from His view. He sees all things and knows all things. We can never go anywhere that is beyond His vision and interest.

"For you formed my inward parts; you knitted me together in my mother's womb. My frame was not hidden from you, when I was being made in secret, intricately woven in the depths of the earth. Your eyes saw my unformed substance; in your book were written, every one of them, the days that were formed for me, when as yet there were none of them" (Psalm 139:13,15,16). If God is able to see

and know a child while still in a mother's womb, how much more is He well acquainted with us and all we do once we are born.

Not only is God's eye always watching, His hand is always moving. God not only sees and knows what is going on, He is also able to intervene in space and time, governing all things for His glory and the ultimate good of His people.

Think of that. God's hand is always moving. He is never idle. Never too tired or fatigued to act on your behalf. Never will you find a time that God is "doing nothing." Never will God have a tough week and wish He could have done more. God is never exhausted. He never grows weary. He never encounters a mountain that is too high and too big for Him to move. His arm is always moving, and it is strong; "You have a mighty arm; strong is your hand, high your right hand." (Psalm 89:13).

When Ruth wandered out into the barley fields of Bethlehem one cool April morning, as the sun came up over the hills to the east, she probably wondered, "How in the world am I going to find my way? How will I find food to glean? How will I find a righteous, God-fearing farmer who will let me gather from the leftovers?" Answer? She will find the right row, the one with Boaz in it, because His eye is always watching and His hand is always moving.

Perhaps you are wondering, "How is this situation going to work out? Where will we find a buyer for our property? How will I find another job? What will the doctor's report say? Will my son or daughter find a godly spouse? Will my aging mom or dad be able to find a place to live? How will we be able to afford an education for our children?" The questions go on and on.

At such times, ponder these words: if Creation was a unique exercise of divine energy causing the world to be, providence is a continued exercise of that same energy whereby the Creator, according to his own will, (a) keeps all creatures in being, (b) involves himself in all events, and (c) directs all things to their appointed end (J.I. Packer, *Concise Theology*, p. 54).

And what is the bottom line behind this theology of providence? "The doctrine of providence teaches Christians that they are never in the grip of blind forces (fortune, chance, luck, fate); all that happens to them is divinely planned, and each event comes as a new summons to trust, obey and rejoice, knowing that all is for one's spiritual and eternal good" (Packer, p. 56).

May His watching eye and moving hand enable you to trust, obey and rejoice!

The Worry Wart's Prayer

May 2009

The expression "worry wart" found its way into usage through, of all things, a comic strip created in 1956 by James Williams called "Our Our Way." It featured a young boy nicknamed "Worry Wart" who, rather than begin plagued by worry himself, caused worry in others. Ever since that comic strip appeared, a "worry wart" has been defined as "one who is inclined to worry excessively and needlessly."

Does that describe you? Do you worry too much (excessively) and without reasonable cause (needlessly)? If your answer is yes, keep reading. If your answer is no and you are married, chances are that your spouse is worried about the fact that you don't worry. So keep reading.

The phrase "the man whom the king delights to honor" appears six times in Esther chapter 6. When we think of "kings" and "honor" we usually think in terms of subjects honoring the king. The lesser honoring the greater. But in the book of Esther, it is the other way around. The king is honoring a certain type of man. The greater is honoring the lesser and surprisingly, the king enjoys doing so. He "delights to honor."

What we have is not the duty of the lesser to honor the greater, but the delight of the greater to honor the lesser. The king gets a big smile on his face when he is honoring another. It is the glory of the king to receive honor, but it is also his glory and joy, perhaps his greater joy, to give honor.

Reading about "the man whom the king delights to honor" made me think of Jesus's words: *For it is your Father's good pleasure to give you the kingdom" (Luke 12:32).* It is elsewhere translated, "Your Father has chosen gladly to give you the kingdom." (NASB). Like a king who delights to honor a man of lesser standing, so God delights and "chooses gladly" to give His kingdom to those of lesser standing, whom He calls His "little flock."

But, what does all this have to do with worry warts? When you read Jesus's words in context you find out that the "little flock" is a flock of worry warts!

> And he said to his disciples, "Therefore I tell you, do not be anxious about your life, what you will eat, nor about your body, what you will put on. For life is more than food, and the body more than clothing. Consider the ravens: they neither sow nor reap, they have neither storehouse nor barn, and yet God feeds them. Of how much more value are you than the birds! And which of you by being anxious can add a single hour to his span of life? If then you are not able to do as small a thing as that, why are you anxious about the rest? Consider the lilies, how they grow: they neither toil nor spin, yet I tell you, even Solomon in all his glory was not arrayed like one of these. But if God so clothes the grass, which

*is alive in the field today, and tomorrow is thrown
into the oven, how much more will he clothe you, O
you of little faith! And do not seek what you are to
eat and what you are to drink, nor be worried. For
all the nations of the world seek after these things,
and your Father knows that you need them. Instead,
seek his kingdom, and these things will be added to
you. "Fear not, little flock, for it is your Father's good
pleasure to give you the kingdom" (Luke 12:22-32).*

What is it that frees a worry wart from excessive and needless worry? What unshackles him or her from the prison house of worry? On what basis does Jesus tell his little flock of worry warts "fear not"? "Fear not, little flock, for (because) it is your Father's good pleasure to give you the kingdom."

There are two reasons that worry warts can let go of their worries and walk safely through life minus the furrowed brow. First, the Father will one day give them the kingdom. Why should we worry excessively and needlessly when God has promised such a positive outcome? Second, why should we worry excessively and needlessly when our Heavenly Father delights to do this? He doesn't grudgingly give us the kingdom. He delights in giving gifts. It makes Him happy to do it! It was His idea.

Let me suggest this worry wart's prayer: Father, unshackle me from the prison of worry. You have promised to one day give me the kingdom and this promise comes with a smile. Why should your smile of delight meet with my fretting face? Free this member of your "little flock" from worry so that your smile of delight is reflected in my smile of belief. Amen.

"Can You Repeat That?"

For many years, on more than one occasion, Lois has shaken her head, rolled her eyes at me and said, "You are a crazy man! You know that, don't you?" The smiling, upturned corners of her mouth assure me in some inexplicable way that she actually kind of enjoys my crazy adventures. But, this time it didn't look like she was smiling.

Help me out. Can you see any problem with the following?

Our family of eight joins the backpacking high school group (70+people) flying to California for the Trinity Alps backpack trip. Derek and Kyle hike with their friends, but the rest of the family (Kate, Jacob, Susie, Luke, mom and dad) will take a simple hike into a nice lake I visited twenty years ago, setting up a base camp for four nights and then hiking out. Hey, let's invite Kate's boyfriend, Ted, who just graduated from college. It can be our graduation present to him. Get to know him better. Family bonding. Grill him with questions late at night. Fun things like that.

After the hike, while the high school group sightsee in San Francisco, we spend the day visiting friends in Orland, where we spent thirteen years in ministry. Then Kate and Ted head back to Chicago for work, everyone else goes to Grandpa and Grandma Krogh's in San Diego for a few days, while Lois and I tour around Northern California/Southern Oregon, seeing the redwoods and stopping at quaint shops (emphasis on quaint, Lois will like that).

We join the family in San Diego, along with my sister, her husband and small children from New Mexico. We now have twelve people, half of which are children, in a medium-to-small sized four-bedroom house. Grandma is worried about their forty-year-old rusted out diving board, but I am sure we can get somebody to fix that before we arrive. What could go wrong?

So, that's about it. Not a crazy plan at all, is it? Once Lois signed off on the plan in general, I started working on the details and discovered the "simple hike" was actually a round trip of nearly twenty miles involving "one of the steepest climbs in the Trinity Alps" rather than the five or six easy miles I had told Lois. (Amazing how the details get hazy over the years!) The redwoods touring would be so much nicer on a motorcycle (think fresh air, majestic views). The chiropractor said he could get most of my back problem straightened out by July. We find out that Kyle needs to be in Fort Wayne, Indiana, for a basketball tournament when we are supposed to be in San Diego.

Sure, there were a few unanswered questions such as: If we ride the big bus with the large group to the airport in Chicago, how do we get back to Hudsonville? How do you get all the backpack stuff and motorcycle stuff into your carry on? Doesn't it rain a lot in the redwoods groves, and if you are on a motorcycle don't you get a little bit...? How do you get from the motorcycle rental to the Sacramento airport? How do you get nine people and backpacks in an eight seat rental vehicle? What does Mom think about Derek and Kyle going out a bit early to climb Mt. Lassen, an active volcano? About that time, I decided to stop asking questions.

So why do I mention all that? Two reasons. First, in case Lois isn't her smiling self when you see her on our return, you will have some background. Second, to ask you to pray for us while we are away.

We look forward to seeing you when we return, with lots of stories to tell!

Three Things I Learned on Vacation

July 2009

Where is my missing motorcycle glove? I had it when I went into the store. Did I drop it in the parking lot? Let's get on our hands and knees on the hot asphalt and look under these cars. Let's retrace our steps down every aisle. Let's ask at customer service, "Did anyone turn in a glove that looks like this?" I bet some lady picked it up and put it in her cart and will turn it in when she checks out. Let's waste half an hour of our vacation waiting to see. Let's walk up and down the aisles looking in people's carts. "Excuse me, just checking to see if you have a left-handed Harley Davidson glove in your cart among the pickles and lunch meats." Why are they giving me strange looks? I leave my name and number at the customer service, asking, "If anyone turns in a glove. . ."

Two hours later and a hundred miles down the road, the cell phone rings. "Mr. Krogh, a lady turned in your glove. Do you want to come and get it?"

"No, that's OK. Could you mail it to my home in Michigan?"

Two days later, the temperature drops from a toasty 100 degrees in Oregon to a cold, damp 56 degrees along the California coast. My ungloved left hand is frozen. Every rider passing me in the opposite direction waves a warm gloved hand at me. My ungloved return salute must make them think, "He is either crazy, from Alaska or lost his glove in the grocery store I passed in Oregon." I don't dare tell Lois that I have lost all fine motor skills in my shifting hand. That would make her nervous, especially on these hairpin turns with no guardrail and a fifty foot cliff.

Lesson One. The next time your kids a) misplace something, b) lose something, c) don't put something away properly, d) slow you down and take up your valuable time through their careless mistakes, e) etc..., smile and remember your frozen left hand. Be patient with them. Mistakes happen. Their father doesn't have it all together either.

We walk into the beautiful, new downtown baseball stadium to watch the San Diego Padres host the Milwaukee Brewers. Not only is it Friday Fireworks Night, it is also "Five for Five Night" meaning mom doesn't need to make dinner and everyone gets a five-course meal (hot dog, soda, peanuts, popcorn, cookie) for $5. I have the bright idea of arriving an hour early so we can watch batting practice. We have seats four rows behind the left field fence. Maybe one of the boys can catch a home run? I am excitedly directing people to their appropriate seats when I hear a collective gasp. I turn around to see my mother doubled over, staggering and reaching out to grasp a seat to steady herself. She is instantly surrounded by ushers, who whisk her to the Red Cross treatment room on the opposite side of the stadium. While I stand there with my mouth hanging open, looking dumbfounded, my eyes saying, "whatintheworldjusthappened?"

Lois mouths to me, "Watch the kids. I will go with your mother."

Turns out that instead of one of the boys catching a homerun ball, a 380 foot line drive hits grandma right above her left hip. The nice Padre people take her blood pressure, give her a Padre backpack (not sure what she will do with that!) a Padre visor and other goodies. The next day she shows me the bruise the size of a grapefruit she also got.

Lesson Two: Part 2a: Always watch out for your parents, especially your mother. The command, "Children, honor your father and mother" doesn't have an expiration date. As parents get older, walk slower. Help them with steps and handrails. Above all else, don't turn your back on them during batting practice. Part 2b: When there is an unexpected accident and someone get hurts, a woman will figure out what's going on, who got hurt and what needs to be done a whole lot faster than a man will. So men, instead of looking stupid, just look to your wife to know what is going on.

We drive past my old high school, which is now in a more diverse neighborhood. We go to see the next "new community." The homes are newer, bigger, nicer. My dad tells me, "This zip code has the highest foreclosure rate in the whole state of California, maybe the nation." House after house is empty. We pass an elementary school I am told, "This school will be closed this fall. Not enough kids. Everyone has moved. This used to be the place to be."

Lesson Three: *"Better is a little where love is, than a fatted ox and strife with it" (Proved 15:17)*. Nothing wrong with enjoying a nice ox tenderloin I suppose, but if it comes with strife, the price is too great. Our culture is always dangling the carrot of the next new thing before us. But, is that where we will truly find happiness? Contentment? Rest? No. Those things come from God.

It was a great vacation. We are happy to be home.

"Much Obliged, Lord"

Fulton Oursler learned the lesson of a grateful heart from an African-American woman who helped care for him when he was a little boy. Every time she sat down to eat, she would bow her head and say, "Much obliged, Lord." Oursler asked her why she did this because the food was there for her to enjoy whether she gave thanks or not. She replied, "Sure we get our vittles, but it makes everything taste better to be grateful. Looking for good things is a kind of game an old preacher taught me to play. Take this morning. I woke up and thought, 'What's there to praise God for today?' You know what? I couldn't think of a thing! Then from the kitchen came the most delicious odor that ever tickled my nose. Coffee! "Much obliged, Lord, for the coffee," I said, "and much obliged, too, for the smell of it.'"

This Thanksgiving season, do you have reason to say, "Much obliged, Lord"? Do you have many things for which to be thankful? Perhaps you wonder what's the big deal about being thankful? Is it really that important?

The apostle Paul lets us know how important thanksgiving is

when he tells us that one of the primary reasons God reveals His wrath against ungodliness and unrighteousness has to do with man's unthankful heart: *"For although they knew God, they did not honor him as God or give thanks to him, but they became futile in their thinking, and their foolish hearts were darkened" (Romans 1:21).*

Jesus reveals how important thanksgiving is when he says to the leper who was healed and fell on his face at Jesus' feet to give Him thanks, "Were not ten cleansed? Where are the nine? Was no one found to return and give praise to God except this foreigner?" (Luke 17:17-18). Giving thanks is equated with giving praise to God.

After a lengthy list of commands instructing us regarding showing compassion, kindness, humility, meekness, patience, forbearance, forgiveness and love, Paul finishes the list with "And be thankful." (Colossians 3:15). Thanksgiving is not a tack-on to the list of commands; thankfulness is the capstone. Being thankful makes everything taste better.

So, what do you have to be thankful for this Thanksgiving season? Do our hearts say, "Much obliged, Lord" about many things or few things.

Here are a few things on my thanksgiving list from recent days:

Lord, much obliged for . . . doctors who take care of ankle sprains, a vacuum that sucks up leaves, a church filled with music, a wife who fears God and loves our children, a bed to sleep in, horseradish sauce, people in our church who love other people, wise counselors, John Piper's book *The Misery of Job and the Mercy of God*, sunlight, a trampoline for my kids and the neighborhood kids, Hager Park, children who are finding their niche in life, choice friends old and new, people who are good at things I am not good at. . . .

Many years later, Fulton Oursler, now a grown man, stood at the bedside of the woman who cared for him as a young boy. As she lay dying in much pain, he wondered if she could still find something to be grateful for. Just then she opened her eyes. As she saw him and the others gathered around, she folded her hands and said with a smile, "Much obliged, Lord, for such fine friends."

The Land of The Red Dust

There are two seasons in Cameroon: rainy season and dry season. I have experienced them both. Let me try to describe them to you.

Rainy season begins in April and runs for six months. When you hear "rainy season" don't think of perpetual mist and gloomy, overcast skies. Think of tropical thunderstorms that appear on the horizon, blow across the mountains and valleys, release their life-giving water at 7,000 feet elevation and leave behind a sky so blue and grass so green that life is so vibrant you can almost touch it and taste it. You may have to run for cover for twenty minutes during the rainy season when the skies let loose, but an hour later, you can enjoy an outdoor picnic as the tropical sun and warmth dries things out nearly instantly. Rainy season in Cameroon in the mountains is a beautiful moment waiting to happen.

Dry season begins in October and lasts until the first showers of April. A fine coat of red dust covers everything, a wind-born result of the expanding Saharan desert that is slowly encroaching south across Africa. Remove the dust from your table at breakfast and when you sit down for dinner, you will find that the dust returned before you did. When you are told, "If you would like to have your shoes polished, please leave then outside your door" you may think, "A daily shoeshine? What a nice touch! I don't get that at home." But you soon realize both why the offer is made and the futility of the task.

If you can't guess which season I prefer, here are a few more hints. Rainy season is life, refreshing, invigorating, at times exhilarating. Dry season is lifeless, draining, tedious, wearying. Rainy season is adventurous. Dry season is monotonous. In rainy season we ask, "When will the thunder come? How fast will the rain come and go? What adventure will happen today?" In the dry season we ask, "Are we done yet? How long, O Lord? This again?" Rainy season points us away from ourselves and asks, "Do you see the colors? Isn't life grand? Isn't God great?" Dry season asks harder questions.

Life has its seasons as well. Which season are you in? If you are enjoying the refreshing rains, I rejoice with you. Isn't God good? When the heavens open and He washes you with grace and undeserved favor, please don't hide your smile. It diminishes the goodness of God if you do. Enjoy the emerald greens and sapphire blues. Plants and skies are gifts from God to be enjoyed with outstretched hands and uplifted faces. Share both the gifts given and your joy in the Giver with others. That is why God has watered His earth and you with the rains of grace.

If you are in the midst of a dry season, let me share two things. First, please know that God is big enough to hear you ask the hard questions. He isn't threatened. Actually, he has heard the same questions from the lips of dear saints who have endured not only dust, but also dungeons, disease and death. Because the questions have been asked before doesn't mean the pain is not real to you or me; it only means that we should ask the questions humbly and with a heart that believes God has and does listen to His people. God is not in a hurry. He doesn't sheepishly paw and toe the dust, and wish He could do something about this dry season, but knows His hands are tied. He makes no apologies for dry seasons. He has His purposes in your life. Ask God to show you what they are. Internal, unseen heart change perhaps happens best among the red dust of life.

Second, know that April rains are coming. Dry season will end one day end and never appear again: *"Neither shall there be mourning nor crying nor pain anymore, for the former things (including red dust) have passed away" (Revelation 21:4).*

Esther Burr, the married daughter of Jonathan Edwards, unexpectedly lost her husband to death at the age of forty-one. Not long after the funeral she faced the prospect of losing her infant son to death because of a horrible infection. Esther wrote her father a precious letter, letting him know that all was well and that God's grace and kindness was wil her through all these difficulties.

As soon as he read his daughter's letter, Jonathan Edwards wrote this surprising letter in return: "Dear Daughter, I thank you for your most comfortable letter. How good and kind is your Heavenly Father! Indeed, he is a faithful God; and never will fail them that trust in him. But don't be surprised, or think some strange thing has happened to you, if after the light, clouds of darkness should return. Perpetual sunshine is not usual in this world, even to God's true saints."

Note Edwards said, "In this world." In this world we do not experience perpetual sunshine, but in the world to come we will! Edwards elsewhere said, "The enjoyment of God is the only happiness with which our souls can be satisfied. To go to heaven, fully to enjoy

God, is infinitely better than the most pleasant accommodations here. Fathers and mothers, husbands, wives, no children, or the company of earthly friends, are but shadows; but God is the substance. These are but scattered beams, but God is the sun.These are but streams. But God is the ocean."

May your dry season and mine cause us to long for the Eternal rains of grace that are fast approaching. May our appetites be whet for the coming freshness of the kingdom that will always be ours, never taken away.

March Madness and Eternal Gladness

Well, it's that time of year again! March Madness. It's time to fill out your NCAA basketball brackets, choosing between teams you have never seen play and know nothing about, yet you announce authoritatively to your children around the dinner table, "Of course UTEP is going to beat VMI, they have more letters!" At our house, some of the women weigh in choosing teams based on the name of the mascot. "I'm picking the Xavier Musketeers to beat the UC Irvine Anteaters." Well, who wouldn't pick a musketeer over an anteater? Talk about obvious!

For those of us who have sons or daughters playing on basketball teams, March Madness also means you now have your life back! Since December our family has been doing our best to make it to two to four games a week, not to mention driving Jake to practice.

When you take in that much basketball, you can't help getting a little philosophical as you get well acquainted with backless bleacher seats. Here are some less-than-significant reflections:

1. Having kids play basketball makes the winter go by faster.

2. The ticket man at Muskegon High is the kindest man in the OK Red when it comes to charging large families, saying, "Wow! Look at all of you! How about $10 for the whole crew, including the grandparents?" He has done that for three years now. Bless you, sir.

3. Speaking of tickets, I have learned that when you drop off the grandparents at curbside and go park the car, if you walk slow enough, by the time you get to the ticket counter Grandpa Krogh will have already paid for the family. Bless you too, sir.

4. Every parent thinks his or her kids should get more playing time. There are more kids than minutes. This creates difficulties. 'Nough said.

5. When you are at an elder meeting and Susie is texting in scores at the end of every quarter, don't jump up and yell and scream. It may not be an appropriate moment for that.

6. I must admit that Hudsonville has a more energetic and creative students cheering section than Jenison, but Jenison's team poster is far superior. Why? Hint: The picture was taken at the Harley dealership.

Now, here is one hopefully significant reflection. Good teams play to their strengths and minimize their weaknesses. Every team has strengths and weaknesses. The teams that play well as a team know their teammates' strengths and know their weaknesses. They play to those strengths and cover for one another's weaknesses.

For example, if your forward is a great rebounder but can't dribble up court if his life depended on it, you get the ball out of his hands as quickly as possible after he cleans the glass. If your guard can't create his own shot but is lights out with a spot-up three, you set a double pick for him and give him a high five when it's nothing but net.

This is rather obvious, but why don't all teams do this? Why is it that some teams manage to pull this off, while others consistently struggle? Perhaps there are many reasons, but I have observed that the teams who play to one another's strengths and minimize one another's weaknesses are teams that have been freed from the tyranny of self and the applause of man because they know for whom they are playing.

What I mean by that is this. The two guys setting the screens don't get their names in the paper or big numbers in the box score, but that doesn't bother them. The guy who brings the ball up the court, and then dishes back to the guy who got the defensive rebound and runs the floor is happy to play to his teammate's strength. The guy who gets knocked silly drawing a charge gets off the floor with a smile.

Why? Because on a good team, players are not playing for themselves or for the people who don't really understand the game. They play for the few who do.

Who does that include? First and foremost, the coach. He understands the game better than the people in the stands. The applause and roar of the crowd are great, but two words from the coach, "Great job!", whispered in your ear mean far more.

How does this apply to us as believers? There is a day coming when the applause of men will fade away and the commendation that matters for eternity will be spoken by the One whose appraisal really counts. Applause is nice. Appreciation has its place. But "well done" spoken by the One who really understands means the most.

Do you know for whom you are playing? Have you been freed

from the tyranny of self, the applause of others, looking good, being somebody, because you know there is a higher court? Whether your "team" is your colleagues at work, your spouse, your family, your ministry team at church, are you freed to play to other's strengths because you are playing for an audience of One?

Take a few minutes to think about what that day will be like when you stand before Christ. What will He say at that moment? What will be His appraisal? What words will echo from His lips and echo for eternity?

"For we must all appear before the judgment seat of Christ, so that each one may receive what is due for what he has done in the body, whether good or evil. Whatever you do, work heartily, as for the Lord and not for men, knowing that from the Lord you will receive the inheritance as your reward. You are serving the Lord Christ. His master said to him, 'Well done, good and faithful servant. You have been faithful over a little; I will set you over much. Enter into the joy of your master'" (2 Cor. 5:10; Col. 3:23,24; Matt 25:21).

Pay Your Taxes. . .Honor the Emperor . . . Fear God

April 2010

It is tax season, and in recent weeks I have been involved in a few discussions regarding how a Christian should respond if legislation passes that uses tax dollars for an immoral purpose. I thought I would share a response, slightly edited, that I shared with someone a few months ago.

Dear Friend,

I certainly am in favor of legislation which prohibits tax dollars being used to fund abortions. Here are my thoughts should a version pass which allows this:

1. *Christians are to pay taxes imposed by the government (Romans 13:1-7). It is hard for me to believe that when Paul wrote these verses that he agreed with all the tax policies of the Roman Empire. I would assume that there were plenty of Roman Empire expenditures with which Paul would have taken moral exception as a follower of Christ. But his command was to pay taxes.*

2. *The Bible clearly teaches that government is to be a moral enterprise; it is to "punish evil and praise good" (1 Peter 2:13-14). So far so good. But, what happens when government gets things mixed up? Scripture recognizes that civil disobedience is appropriate for believers when either or both of the following happens.*

    a. *When the government commands you to do what the Bible prohibits (i.e. when the government commanded bowing before an idol, God's people refused. [Dan.3]).*
    b. *When the government prohibits you from doing what the Bible commands (when told not to teach in Christ's name, Peter said, "We must obey God rather than man." [Acts 5:29]).*

If you were to ask me, "If the proposed bill becomes law and part of my taxes will be used to pay for abortions, will you engage in civil disobedience/refuse to pay your taxes?" my answer would be: I don't believe that being commanded to pay taxes which are used for immoral purposes rises to the level of directly commanding me to do what the Bible prohibits or prohibiting me from doing what the Bible commands. The Roman Emperor, the U.S. president, the congress, the governing official stand responsible before God for how those taxes are used. Thus, civil disobedience is not justifiable in this instance.

As a citizen of this nation, I have several ways to address my concern regarding an immoral use of taxes: write my congressman, support different legislation, support a political candidate, write a letter to the editor, put a sign in my front yard or on my car bumper, run for office, encourage a godly and wise person to run for office, pray. But, at the end of the day, I need to pay my taxes.

What if someone is convinced otherwise? What if a Christian concludes that when the government demands payment of taxes which are used for immoral purposes, it does rise to a level of justified civil disobedience? Though I differ with this conclusion, I would encourage the person to think through two things.

First, it seems to me that you cannot withhold paying all taxes because you have an objection of conscience regarding how a portion of the texes is used. Determining which portion/percentage not to pay seems to be a very difficult course of action.

Second, when a person engages in an act of civil disobedience, he or she needs to be prepared to suffer the consequences, i.e. receive whatever penalty or punishment may be meted out. This is no small matter. I learned first-hand years ago when I participated in an Operation Rescue at an abortion clinic in California that the government does not bear the sword in vain. My so-called day in court was a miscarriage of justice, and ultimately I was sentenced to 200 hours of community service. As I "did my time" on my one day off a week for seven months, I had plenty of time to think through the cost of civil disobedience. Christians who engage in civil disobedience should not be naive about what they are doing. When the gavel comes down, the judge and court officials go home to enjoy their families and barbecues, losing little sleep over the "conscientious objectors" that appeared that day in court.

To conclude, far from being an exercise in mental gymnastics, I think we will see the day when we will need great wisdom in such matters. Churches may face the dilemma of losing their tax-exempt status for upholding biblical teaching and practice. Financial consequences could be immense. Likewise, even careful and thoughtful pastors may face accusations that their sermons contain "hate speech."

Rather than living in fear of such days, may we have the wisdom of Jesus who caused his questioners to marvel when he said, "Render to Caesar the things that are Caesar's, and to God the things that are God's. (Mark 12:17). May we all do as Peter commanded: *"Honor everyone. Love the brotherhood. Fear God. Honor the emperor"* (1 Peter 2:17).

"Who Gives This Woman?" (Part One)

June 2010

In thirty-four days, I need to give the answer to that question! Many of you have already uttered these life-changing words that no father says lightly. This will be a first for me.

Let me offer some observations that hopefully will strike a chord with dads who have already given their daughters in marriage and prepare my fellow dads for their daughters' big day. I will take the question in reverse order, starting with the last words and working back to the beginning of the question.

"This Man." Now that's a good question to start with! Just who is "this guy" and how did he get into this story starring my daughter and her favorite leading man—me, her dear old dad?

I hope you as a father know who he is. You have talked with him, his parents, his siblings, his pastor. You have asked him questions and listened to his answers. You have observed him in his element and you have invited him into yours. You have heard his dreams for life and you have shared your dreams for your daughter. As you do this, I think there are two key questions to discern.

First, which direction is he headed? Is he moving toward Christ and His Kingdom or is he moving toward his own smaller agenda? Is he striding toward things eternal or is he living for the here-and-now? Is he moving forward in loving God supremely and loving others sacrificially, or is he yet to shred the wrapper of loving self?

How do you find out these things? It takes open eyes and ears. Ask questions and listen for the answers. Call his pastor and ask him the questions that are important to you. If possible, meet his parents. Then invite the young man on a four-day backpack trip with your entire family and have him sleep in the same small tent with your youngest two sons. Yes, the ones with the stinky feet. You will quickly know the answers to lots of questions.

Second, besides figuring out which direction he is headed, since he wants to be your daughter's husband, not just your backpacking partner, you need to know where he stands in relation to her. To be specific: Is he able to be her spiritual leader and physical provider?

Spiritually speaking, who will be following whom in this marriage? Is he committed to Christ and His church? How has he shown that? For how long? Has your daughter become more settled (in a good way) since meeting him? Does he know his way around the Word? Being able to find Obadiah is a definite plus, but more importantly, has the Sermon on the Mount found a way into his heart?

Practically speaking, is he a provider? When did he get his first job? What is he doing now and how long has he been doing it? Does he know how to manage money?

So what if all is good with this man? What if he's headed in the right direction and is able to be your daughter's spiritual leader and practical provider? If his only glaring problem is that he is young, get over it. Quite likely when you look at your own wedding pictures, you will say like me, "How in the world did they let these two people get married so young?"

What if you have reservations? Before talking with your daughter, talk with someone you respect and trust. Make sure you are reading things right and are able to communicate things well, speaking the truth in love.

To all the daughters who may be reading this article, listen to your dad! If he loves God, loves the Word and loves you—I beg you to listen to his concerns. Maybe he sees something you don't. If you think your dad and mom are being unfair or misguided, talk it through. Be patient. Listen. Get an outside evaluation by someone who knows you and you respect. Talk to a spiritual mentor or pastor.

"To Be Married." Marriage isn't about just a wedding ceremony. Speaking of weddings, they cost a lot! Every family is different. I encourage you to 1) Talk to others to get a ballpark figure. 2) Figure out what is appropriate for your family's station in life. 3) Give that amount to the future newlyweds, and let them have the joy and struggle of making it all work.

More importantly, marriage is about making covenant vows and keeping them. Make sure the person doing their premarital counseling understands the importance of vows. Tell your daughter and fiance that fidelity to their vows is more important than career, house size, car they drive, the number of kids they have or vacations they take. Tell them that you will be praying for their mutual faithfulness to those vows.

Let them know that you think marriage is a good thing. It is humbling at times, but it is good. As a dad, the greatest gift you can now give your daughter is letting her future husband see what loving a wife looks like. Let him see that you enjoy the wife of your youth a few decades on. (Ecclesiastes 9:9). Let him see that you wear the mantle of a servant-leader and provider without complaining about it. Let him know that you truly believe that Jesus said, "It is more blessed to give than to receive." (Acts 20:35).

Be honest and tell them of when you had to apologize in your marriage. Use discretion, but be real. If you tell them your shortcomings before they are married, they are much more likely to seek your wisdom and prayers in the future.

I didn't finish all my thoughts on this question. Guess that will have to wait until next time when there will be only six days left until the big day!

"Who Gives This Woman?" (Part Two)

Only six days until I answer the question, "Who gives this woman to be married to this man?" Kate is hoping I can choke out the right answer despite the lump that will be in my throat. I can hear her saying, "Focus Dad. Focus. Only four words. You can do this."

I have offered some observations on this important question that the father of the bride is asked. I took the question in reverse order focusing on the last two parts "this man" and "to be married". Today we look at the first two parts "this woman" and "who gives."

"This Woman." Let me share some thoughts for dads, and then for daughters. Yes, dads, our little girls do grow up! I can remember when Katie went away to college and announced, "From now on I am going to have people call me Kate." I found out that I was one of those people! Not only do names change, so do relationships.

One of the most influential relationships in your daughter's life is her relationship with you, her dad. As a young girl becomes a young woman and bride-to-be, what are some key ingredients in a healthy, maturing, dad-daughter relationship? Let me offer three.

First, one way a girl becomes a young lady is by her father treating her as one. Look for opportunities to involve your daughter in your life in ways that show that you are honoring her femininity (1 Peter 3:7). I can remember a time that I took Katie, uh, Kate, on a trip to Philadelphia for a conference I was attending. She sat through many of the sessions of the conference, catching bits and pieces along the way, but we had the opportunity to enjoy a concert one evening and do a historical walking tour of Philadelphia by flashlight another evening.

More recently, I shared a train adventure with Susannah, giving me the opportunity to teach her how to engage in conversation with strangers. I also had plenty of opportunity to listen to Susie talk, which she is quite good at!

Simple things like opening the door for your daughter when you go to Wolfgang's for breakfast or holding her hand when you walk the pier in Grand Haven do not go unnoticed. Young girls grow to be secure, poised ladies when they know their fathers seek out and enjoy their company.

Second, along with the many yeses to your daughter, don't be afraid to say no. Just as David lacked the strength to say no to his son Adonijah (1 Kings 1:6), sometimes it is difficult for a father to risk displeasing his daughter. After you have listened, asked questions, discussed and listened some more, if the answer needs to be no, then you need to say no. I can remember two critical occasions when an important decision did not turn out the way Kate wished. Daughters, like all our children, need to learn that life does not revolve around them, nor does their every desire become reality. They need to learn that though their dad loves them, he is subject to following God's leading in his life and his family's life.

My experience has been that, by the grace of God, your daughter will thank you, perhaps years later, for having the strength to give a loving and firm no as needed.

Third, your daughter is unique and one-of-a-kind. No two people are alike, including your own daughters. Your daughter is going to be different from your wife. One may be a worry-wart, concerned about the details, while the other is carefree and has a "don't sweat the details" approach.

Make it your goal to understand your daughter. What unique strength has God given her? What relational skills does she have? How can you help her flourish and become the person God designed her to be? Your care for her in this way will mean much to her.

Now, a quick word to daughters. One of the ways you can honor your father is to thank him for his care for you. Dads tend to have a lot on their plate and often feel like they're spinning those plates on a stick, trying to keep everything from crashing. We get consumed with fixing problems. If your dad seems distracted and distant at times, just grab him by the hand, look in his eyes and say, "Dad, I just want to thank you for taking care of me." Even better, if and when he says no to you, accept that as God's no and ask Him to give you a trusting and submissive heart.

"Who Gives." One of the things I have learned in this wedding countdown is that the bride's family is giving up more than the groom's family. No offense to Kate's fiance, Ted, and the entire Cockle clam, but there is a reason the father of the bride is asked for his permission for his daughter to be married. Her change of surname is more than just words. It is a change of family relationship. She is becoming part of his family more than he is becoming part of yours.

At first glance you may say, wait a minute. That's not right. Each family is gaining. One family is gaining a daughter, the other is gaining a son. Yes, but there is a little bit more to it than that. Why is she changing her last name? Why does the Bible speak consistently of sons taking a wife and a daughter being given in marriage and never the other way around? Why does the Bible say, "Therefore a man shall leave his father and his mother and hold fast to his wife, and they shall become one flesh." (Gen 2:24), with the man as the initiator?

Or put it this way, imagine a Mr. Lockerbie, who has two sons that marry. If each son is blessed with four daughters who in turn are married, how long will the Lockerbie family name continue? It ceases with his two sons, while those eight granddaughters become part of the heritage of other families.

Don't get me wrong, if and when my sons marry, the shoe will be on the other foot. When my daughter-in-law's father is asked, "Who gives this woman . . . " I will have a lump in my throat then too, because he is giving away his life and soul, his flesh and blood. He is giving away his precious daughter whom he has loved, protected, and cared for. If you ask me at that moment, "Who is getting the better part of this arrangement?" I will say, "The Kroghs are."

What is the point of this? Dads, God wants you to protect and provide for your daughter. She "belongs" to you in the good sense of that word. Does she sense that? Does she feel prized by you? Does she feel that whoever is fortunate enough to get a yes from you when asked for her hand in marriage is one blessed man? As she grows up, when it comes to attracting the interest of men, encourage her not to be the low-hanging fruit on the branches, accessible to all passersby. Let her know that the best fruit is higher up on the tree, harder to reach but worth the effort.

Then, when the big day comes and you give her away to be married, realize that you are really giving her away. When she changes her name, she also changes her allegiances. Encourage her to be Mrs. Cockle now. Encourage her to honor her husband, as she once honored you. She will know you will be around for wisdom and counsel as needed, but let her know that you are confident that her husband will now provide love and godly leadership in her marriage.

Those are the thoughts that I will be bouncing around in my head in a week. I hope the right words will come out of my mouth.

"Do You Believe This?"

When I left the church one night, I nodded at a friend and said as I left the room, "See you later." Little did he or I know, that "later" would mean in glory. A few hours later I received a phone call that he had passed away. In the inky darkness of 3:00 a.m., I stood in his home, hugging the members of his family, whose lives would never be the same.

At times like that, one of the questions you ask is, "Do I believe what I say I believe?" When Martha's brother, Lazarus, died, Jesus said to Martha, "I am the resurrection and the life. Whoever believes in me, though he die, yet shall he live, and everyone who lives and believes in me shall never die" (John 11:25, 26a). Perhaps you can quote those words from memory, but do you know what Jesus said next? He asked Martha, "Do you believe this?" (John 11:26b).

Pretend that you are Martha, grieving for your brother. Or maybe you don't need to pretend, you know what it is like. Jesus asks you, "Do you believe this?" Do you really believe that Jesus is the resurrection and the life and all who believe in Him will live forever? Do you really believe that the grave is not the end? Do you really believe that as believers in Christ, even if we taste death, yet shall we live? Do you really believe that your "Lazarus", be it husband, wife, brother, sister, son, daughter, friend, even if they die shall live?

There are many reasons I find it credible and rational to believe that Jesus is the resurrection and the life, and has power over death. These reasons include the historicity of the New Testament documents, the testimony of eyewitnesses of the Risen Christ (some of whom were martyred for their testimony), the specific and precise prophecies regarding the nature and timing of Christ's birth, death and resurrection, which were recorded centuries before Jesus. Really, it is quite reasonable to believe what Jesus told Martha is true: Jesus is the resurrection and the life and all who believe in Him will live forever.

However, my aim is not to defend the resurrection and the life. My question is not, is it believable, but do you believe it? If I really believe this, my life will be different in several ways.

1. My life will be different in the way I *grieve*. Believing that Jesus is the resurrection and the life does not mean that I don't cry over the death of someone I love. It does not mean that my tears are absent; it means that my tears are different. *"But we do not want you to be uninformed, brothers, about those who are asleep (i.e., dead) that you may not grieve as others do, who have no hope" (1 Thes. 4:13).* My tears speak of hurt. I mourn. I feel loss and pain. Death is an enemy. My tears also speak of hope. One day all tears will be wiped away. One day the dead in Christ will rise. One day we will be caught up together with them to meet the Lord. One day I will see my Savior along with those who loved him.

2. My life will be different in the way I *give*. Jim Elliot, the missionary speared to death in the jungle of Ecuador, wrote

these words in his diary, "He is no fool who gives us what he cannot keep to gain that which he cannot lose." Believing that Jesus is the resurrection and the life, knowing that the grave is not the end, frees a person to be a giver. For Jim Elliot the question was not all that difficult: Will I hold on to things I will have to let loose of one day, or will I let them go so that I can take hold of things eternal?

3. My life will be different in the way I **_grow older_**. Recognizing that Jesus is the resurrection and the life means that we know He is the final arbiter. It is His appraisal that will last for eternity. We need not live in fear of others' evaluation of us. We should not crave or live for the approval of men. Nor should we naively think our self-perceptions are without error. Paul said, *"Therefore, do not pronounce judgment before the time, before the Lord comes, who will bring to light the things in darkness and will disclose the purposes of the heart. Then each one will receive his commendation from God" (1 Cor. 4:5).* Knowing that the resurrected Christ is the One before whom I will stand one day is both liberating and humbling. It liberates me from the tyranny of trying to please everyone. It liberates me from the gangrene of self-pity when I am wronged, slandered or misunderstood. It liberates me from bitterness when I suffer injustice. But, with this liberty comes the humility of knowing I will give an account to Him who sees all things, including the motives of my heart. Paul said, *"I am not aware of anything against myself, but I am not thereby acquitted. It is the Lord who judges me" (1 Cor. 4:4).*

Jesus, who is the Resurrection and the Life, asks you, "Do you believe this?" Hopefully, your life shows that you do.

Speaking Like Christ

There are many facets to being like Christ in our conduct. I have been thinking lately about being like Christ in our conversations, specifically in the way he spoke to the Samaritan woman at the well in John 4.

Jesus said to her, *"Go, call your husband, and come here." The woman answered him, "I have no husband." Jesus said to her, "You are right in saying, 'I have no husband'; for you have had five husbands, and the one you now have is not your husband. What you have said is true" (John 4:14-18).*

Jesus begins and ends this conversation with grace and kindness: "You are right" and "What you have said is true." Imagine what it meant to hear Jesus affirm and agree with this woman who had known heartache and upheaval in her relationships. Think how often she must have heard, "No. You are wrong. I am right. You don't know what you are talking about." How sweet it was for Jesus' affirming words to echo in her soul.

Being Christ-like means we look for ways to affirm and agree with others. "You are right! What you have said is so true" are words we should often speak. Rather than wanting to prove our point and show others we are right, we should look for ways to agree and affirm what others say.

Try disarming someone this week by listening, and then agreeing and affirming them as much as possible. In doing so, you will spread the fragrance of Christ. If you have a rocky relationship with someone, perhaps a family member, spouse or co-worker, look for ways to say, "You are right!" Say it more than once. Nod in agreement. Give them verbal and non-verbal affirmation. Go out of your way to look for ways to agree with the person rather than pull at the thread of minor disagreements.

However, Jesus did not shy away from saying difficult things: "For you have had five husbands, and the one you now have is not your husband." Hard words to say and hear! Yet Jesus spoke them because He way trying to help the woman see the brokenness and emptiness of the cistern from where she had been drinking. He was "speaking the truth in love" (Eph. 4:15), in "compassion, kindness, humility, meekness, and patience" (Col 3:12). Because these hard words were spoken in a context of patient listening, verbalized affirmation and care, they were received by the Samaritan woman, who eventually told her community, *"Come, see a man who told me all that I ever did. Can this be the Christ?" (John 4:29).*

Part of being Christ-like means that we will gently say pointed, difficult things rather than avoiding them. As you seek to affirm and say with genuineness, "You are right!" as much as possible, also be willing to speak the truth in love when necessary. Be specific, but be concise. We don't need to go on and on belaboring the point. When Jesus spoke the truth in love, he spoke only 16 words.

Imagine how your home would change if you became more like Christ in your conversations, speaking words of affirmation and agreement whenever possible and speaking the truth in love wherever necessary. Imagine how your relationship with friends and family would benefit from your words of affirmation and your willingness to gently address the difficult subjects.

One final thought. What if you are the one being spoken to instead of doing the speaking? How do you respond when someone speaks the truth in love to you? Rather than being defensive, what if you patiently listened and learned? Rather than trying to explain away the current situation, what if your responded with, "You are right. What you have said is true."? You may not only gain a friend, you may also find that the cup of repentance is filled with living water.

Marginal Coffee, Good Pastries, Great Book: Lessons from Bonhoeffer

March 2011

Several of us gathered on a not-too-snowy night at the end of February for our winter reading club book discussion of *Bonhoeffer*. We enjoyed a lively discussion, drank sub-standard coffee (I made it) and ate excellent pastries (I picked what I liked hoping there would be left overs). Let me share with you three Bonhoeffer quotes that deeply impacted me about three different topics.

First the topic of grace. "The preaching of grace can only be protected by the preaching of repentance." Bonhoeffer wrote these words in a paper addressed to the Confessing Church in Germany in 1937 regarding the well-intentioned, but misplaced, dialogue of the ecumenical movement with Hitler and the national Reich church.

What would Bonhoeffer say to the church in America today? Have we preached up grace but preached down repentance? Have we got the part of the good news correct regarding what Christ has done to bear our sin on the cross, but have made things fuzzy about our response to that good news? Have we unwisely separated trusting in Christ and turning from sin? Can you really do the former without the later?

The apostle Paul said of the Thessalonians' conversion experience: *"You turned to God from idols to serve the living and true God"* (1 *Thes. 1:9)*. "Turning to God" (trust and belief) went hand in hand with turning "from idols" (repentance). Surely we would tell nationals in the remote villages of Africa or South America, "Hey, you can't just add a statue of Christ to the other amulets, charms and idols on your table at home!" They need to turn from their idols and turn to Christ. Nor should we allow people in our culture to believe in Jesus without turning from their sins and substitutes for God. The preaching of grace must be protected by the preaching of repentance.

Second, "The essence of Christianity is not about religion at all, but about the person of Christ." I love preaching through one of the gospels because of how we see Jesus as a person who relates to us, speaks to us, befriends us. John closes his gospel, "Now there are also many other things that Jesus did. Were every one of them to be written, I suppose that the world itself could not contain the books that would be written." Perhaps that is part of what eternity will be all about, the full disclosure of the glory of Christ. Bonhoeffer wrote, "It is the nature of Christ to be at the center." We look forward to Him being at His rightful place for all eternity. Is Christ at the center of your life now?

Third, the Incarnation, the fact that we have bodies and that God the Son took on human flesh and walked this earth, was important to Bonhoeffer: "Incarnation led him to the idea that the Christian life must be modeled. Jesus did not only communicate ideas and concepts and rules and principles for living. He lived. And by living with his disciples, he showed them what life was supposed to look like, what God intended it to look like. It was not merely intellectual or merely spiritual. It was all these things together; it was something more. This led him to the idea that to be a Christian, one must live with Christians."

How are you living with other Christians? How about the ones who are different than you? Or the ones that disappointed you or hurt you? How about those who have needs? *"Love is patient and kind; love does not envy or boast; it is not arrogant, or rude. It does not insist on its own way; it is not irritable or resentful; it does not rejoice at wrongdoing, but rejoices with the truth. Love bears all things, believes all things, hopes all things, endures all things"* (1 Cor. 13:4-7). Who is God asking you to love?

Finally, I close with these moving words about Dietrich Bonhoeffer, from the camp doctor that watched him go to the gallows for what he believed in. "In the almost fifty years that I worked as a doctor, I have hardly ever seen a man die so entirely submissive to the will of God." May we too find the joy and peace of such submission.

The Danger of Assuming the Gospel: The Lesson of Les Mis

April 2011

Stunned silence. How could I be forty-some years old and have never heard before of *Les Miserables*, the incredible story of justice, redemption, law and grace written in 1862 by VIctor Hugo? I sat in stunned silence as the music played at the end of the screen adaptation of Hugos' fabulous drama.

Years later, when I heard the live stage performance of *Les Mis* was coming to Detroit, Lois and I got tickets, invited friends and settled in for an enjoyable evening of theater.

As the play ended, I again sat in stunned silence. This new and revised musical version of *Les Mis* totally missed the drama of redemption, the tension of law and grace, and the marvel of undeserved forgiveness. Instead, the focus was on secondary issues: the French Revolution, the bawdiness of sin. The cast featured fantastic singers; the orchestra pit resonated with incredible music; the scenery and staging were incredible; the special effects jaw-dropping. But the story line was assumed. The director assumed everybody already knew the story, so it didn't need to be re-told.

As everyone applauded and filed out, I felt empty. *You missed it,* I thought. Then, in deeper silence, it hit me: this is what often happens in church today. The storyline of the gospel is assumed. "We already know the story of Christ's incarnation, death, atonement and resurrection," the leaders think. "No need to go there."

When that happens, we are left with what? Music, special effects, dazzling technology, platform personalities. Or even worse, we are left with the pastor's latest spin on secondary issues which become the main thing: be it clean drinking water in Africa or saving the environment or rescuing our schools or fill-in-the-blank.

Does that mean I am in favor of off-key music, worn-out and retreaded methods and dull sermons without cultural relevance? Of course not.

What I hoped for when I travelled to the Fisher Theater in Detroit was that among the lights, music, drama and staging, the main thing would be the main thing. Grace, forgiveness, redemption mercy all intersecting the human heart at center stage. At the end of three hours, I wanted to sit in the stunned silence of God's mercy to me a sinner. Instead there was smoke and mirrors and lesser things.

I hope that when we travel to church every Sunday, you and I will settle for nothing less than the amazing story we think we already fully know. We need to hear the main thing, the good news of the gospel, with freshness and power. We need to plumb the depths of immeasurable grace. Our jaws need to drop in amazement each week: "Can you believe it? God has mercied me, a sinner!"

How will we know if we experience the stunned silence of amazing grace? How will we know if we are captured by the storyline of the gospel? I think there are tangible ways to measure that, including such things as what we put in the offering plate, how we live when we scatter to schools and ball diamonds and newspaper routes and neighborhoods and workplaces and doctor's offices. How we speak to others, how we extend love and hope, how we treat our spouse.

All those things come, not from a gospel that is assumed, but from a gospel that is re-experienced week in and week out, each Sunday in word, worship and community. I trust that we keep the main thing the main thing and that we, the real "miserable ones," are reminded of the mercy God has shown us, the mercy we are now called to show to others and the mercies-to-come which will be ours for all eternity.

Blindness and Tough Love

Recently I watched the classic film *The Miracle Worker*, the dramatic portrayal of how Anne Sullivan gave her pupil Helen Keller the gift of love and the ability to communicate.

In many ways the film is painful to watch, as one agonizes not only for Helen and her parents, but also for Anne Sullivan, Helen's teacher. In one moving scene Anne asks Helen's parents to leave the dining room so that she can strip Helen of her selfish table manners and help Helen to respect her family, which in so doing will restore Helen's dignity and humanity. As I watched the titanic tug-of-war between a child's iron-will obstinacy and a teacher's granite-firm resolve to conquer that child's will, more than once I thought, *Enough already! Get this scene over. I get the point.* By the end of the scene, a dining room is destroyed, but Helen is on her way to being set free.

Anne knows that to complete her task, she needs absolute authority over blind, deaf and mute Helen. She asks Helen's parents to give her this authority to live alone with Helen in a separate location for an extended period of time. Having no other alternative, Helen's parents reluctantly acquiesce.

Once Helen realizes she has been left alone with Anne, who she abhors, she does all she can to make her teacher's life as hellish as her own. Again, it is painful to watch as Helen's blind rage and anger is unleashed on her teacher. Anne endures in her "tough love," knowing that Helen's will must be conquered so she can fully be set free, not just from the captivity of blindness and deafness, but from an even greater tyranny.

A life-changing breakthrough comes when Helen is able to bridge the chasm between the letters "w-a-t-e-r" in sign-language to her fingertips and the actual reality of water gushing from the pump at her home. When letters and words connect with the things signified, new dimensions and vistas immediately open up to her. In many ways, she is blind and deaf no more.

Now, let me add a couple of pastoral observations. First, a word for parents: "tough love" moments are painful, but they are a gift of God as they provide an opportunity for us to wean our children from themselves. After you have communicated your love and care, don't be afraid to say no. Parental resolve comes from knowing what your child really needs: to be freed from the tyranny of self and pride, from the deception that life revolves around them and that their greatest need is happiness.

What do you do if you are in the middle of a titanic tug-of-war with your child? Cry out to God for wisdom, strength and love. Ask God for wisdom to see the big picture, what is really at stake, as well as wisdom for the specific situation. Ask God for strength to outlast your child's iron will. Ask God for supernatural love, as unyielding firmness is melded with undeserved kindness.

Second a word to all of us. Has the God who said, "Let light shine out of darkness," shone into your heart "to give the light of the knowledge of the glory of God in the face of Christ?" (2 Cor. 4:6). Spiritually speaking, can you say, "I once was blind, but now I see?" At one time were you blind to the glory of Christ, but now do you love Jesus and bow before Him as Lord and Savior?

When Anne Sullivan breaks through into Helen's deaf and dark heart, giving her love and light and language for her soul, you want to thank Anne for her resoluteness and perseverance. Likewise, we who now see the beauty and glory of Christ, should thank our Heavenly Father for His resolute and persevering love. His love did not let us go. His resolution brought us freedom from tyranny of self, sin and blindness.

We will have all eternity to thank God for spelling g-r-a-c-e onto our souls. May our lives of obedience and love be the expression of thanks even now.

King for a Day

Have you ever tried to write a proverb? It's not that easy. King Solomon spoke 3,000 proverbs, plus more than 1,000 songs (1 Kings 4:32)! Well, I am no king, but let me offer two proverbs that I apparently composed in my sleep since I woke up today with these two proverbs on my mind.

"If you don't have a horse in the race, wear a nice hat." Not sure what inspired this proverb. Perhaps it's our plan to go to Louisville, Kentucky, this summer on our family vacation to tour a thoroughbred racehorse farm and the Louisville Slugger Bat Factory and Museum for our budding nine-year-old baseball playing Luke.

So what does the proverb mean? If you need a hint, try this slightly different version: "If you don't have a dog in the fight, have a nice day." Ready for the explanation?

Sometimes in life people take on responsibilities that God hasn't given them. King David said, *"O LORD, my heart is not lifted up; my eyes are not raised too high; I do not occupy myself with things too great and too marvelous for me" (Psalm 131:1).* The NASB says:

"Nor do I involve myself in great matters, or in things too difficult for me."

If King David knew some things were beyond the scope of what God gave him to be concerned with, how much more so with us! What causes us to take on matters that God hasn't given us? According to King David: pride. A "lifted up heart" and "eyes raised too high."

Are you over-responding to something that God hasn't placed within your realm of responsibility? Are you rendering your appraisal and judgment, when God hasn't put the case on your docket? Are you being overly dramatic, when your opinion wasn't even requested? Could it be that your pride is causing you to overreach? Are you wearing yourself and others out by worrying about things over which you have no control or responsibility?

Instead what should you do? Wear a nice hat! Enjoy the sun! Have a nice day! Life is difficult enough without taking on concerns outside of our God-given sphere of responsibility. Realize and take comfort in the fact that there are some problems that God will not hold you responsible to solve. He has other people working on those things.

Smile and be glad that there are lofty matters God hasn't assigned you to figure out. Uneasy lies the head that wears the crown. Sleep well, knowing that God hasn't called you to be the king. Instead of a king's crown, enjoy wearing a nice hat!

A second proverb: ***"Strive to be full of grace and truth, but remember which comes first in the alphabet."*** When Jesus walked this earth, He was a perfect combination of grace and truth: *"The Word became flesh and dwelt among us, and we have seen his glory, glory as of the only Son from the Father, full of grace and truth." (John 1:14).* He was able to perfectly blend grace and truth, saying to the woman caught in adultery, "Neither do I condemn you (grace). . . .now go, and sin no more (truth)."

The woman at the well was drawn to Jesus because He perfectly combined grace with truth. Along with hearing truth in what he said, she experienced grace in how he said it. She saw grace in His eyes and heard it in His voice.

Notice what John states: *"And from his fullness we have all received, grace upon grace. For the law was given through Moses; grace and truth came through Jesus Christ." (John 1:16,17).*

Grace upon grace. Grace and truth. Without sacrificing truth, it seems that what separated Jesus from others is that He was able to give proper primacy to grace.

Are you giving proper primacy to grace? Is there an attractiveness to your life that comes from grace? Do others hear words of truth from you, or do they hear truth spoken in grace? Grace causes your circle of influence with others to grow larger and deeper with time. Truth, without grace, causes that circle to shrink and shrivel.

Thanks for reading my two proverbs. It was fun to be king for a day.

Thankfulness: God's Will for Luke's Life and Yours

Lois' mother's heart let her know that our youngest son needed some help in developing a thankful spirit. At the beginning of the school year, Lois gave ten-year-old Luke the following assignment: Every Monday you need to write a list of ten things for which you are thankful. By the end of school, you will have 300 things on that list.

Please know that this was not Luke's idea of a good time. But as the weeks went by, more than once Luke would inform me, "Dad, do you know what I am thankful for this week? Let me tell you. . . " Since this is Thanksgiving month, I thought I would check in with Luke and, with his permission, here are some entries from his list in no particular order..

#11 Our dog that chases deer

#19 Having a campfire outside

#31 Boys Club

#40 Joyful Noise children's choir

#43 Playing Airsoft with Jacob

#45 My poison ivy going away

#52 The first day of snow when it comes

#58 Funny birthday cards to give to my family

#82 Carving pumpkins with friends

#92 Backpacking trips with my family

When I read that Luke was thankful for his poison ivy going away, it made me think of the story about Charles Spurgeon, who learned to be thankful in all circumstances. One day he was robbed on the streets of London. When he arrived home he told his wife, Susannah, about his harrowing experience, concluding with, "Well, thank the Lord anyway." Susannah replied, "Thank the Lord that somebody stole your money?"

"No my dear," answered her husband. He then began to list some reasons why he was thankful. "First, I'm thankful the robber took just my money and not my life. Second, I'm thankful I had left most of our money home and he didn't really rob me of much. Third, I am thankful to God that I was not the robber."

Scripture tells us to *"Rejoice always, pray without ceasing, give thanks in all circumstances; for this is the will of God in Christ Jesus for you" (1 Thes. 5:16-18).* In all circumstances! Including poison ivy or robbery.

Someone gave this definition of thanksgiving: "Nothing taken for granted. Everything received with gratitude. Everything passed on with grace." Did you notice: nothing. . .everything. . . everything? "Give thanks in all circumstances; for this is the will of God in Christ Jesus for you."

Nearly one hundred years after Charles Spurgeon, another preacher in London, Martyn Lloyd-Jones, spoke these words in a sermon: "Surely praise and thanksgiving are ever to be the great characteristics of the Christian life. Praise distinguishes the Christian particularly in his prayer and in his worship. The highest point of all worship and prayer is adoration and praise and thanksgiving."

As Luke prepares to break into the triple digits on his thanksgiving list, I must say that I have noticed a change in his demeanor. He is more pleasant to be around. Much more positive and enjoyable. Much more . . . thankful. My conclusion is that cultivating a thankful heart is not only the right thing to do, it is good for us.

Perhaps we should all begin our own lists. If you begin this week and list ten things you are thankful for, by Christmas you will have eighty and by Easter you will be well into the triple digits!

It might even help your disposition when #52 on Luke's list comes and lasts four months!

What Has God Given You?

"Lord, you have given me so much. Give me one thing more. A grateful heart." So said George Herbert, a godly pastor and poet from generations ago.

As we approach the Thanksgiving season, it is appropriate to reflect on what the Lord has given us. What has God given you?

Perhaps the first thing we think of is *salvation*. An elderly woman once came to Charles Spurgeon, the British preacher, and said, "Ah, Mr. Spurgeon, if Jesus Christ does save me, he shall never hear the end of it." Isn't that beautiful? If Christ has saved you, He should never hear the end of it! What if you began each day, rising to tell the Risen Christ, "You have saved me, Lord. I am so thankful. Thank You for bearing my sin upon Your shoulders. By Your stripes I am healed. Through Your blood, I am made clean. Thank You, Lord."?

When you worship each Sunday morning, is that thought foremost in your mind? Martyn Lloyd-Jones, the Welsh preacher, said, "The highest point of all worship and prayer is adoration and praise and thanksgiving." I find it interesting that he included thanksgiving right along with adoration and praise. Adoration and praise has to do with recognition of who God is. Thanksgiving is your response to what God has done for you in particular. Come next Sunday with a thankful heart for what God has done in saving you from your sins.

Second, we should thank God for His *providence*. "God's works of providence are his most holy, wise, and powerful preserving and governing all His creatures, and all their actions" (Westminster Shorter Catechism Q. 11). God providentially involves Himself in all events and directs all things to their appointed end.

Many times we only see God's providence in the rearview mirror, after an event takes place. A while ago, Lois and I drove to Ann Arbor to help her dad purchase a more suitable vehicle for him to ride in. To make a long story short: the vehicle was not correctly described on the dealer website, the ensuing conversation took so much time that when Lois finally handed over the check her father's bank was closed and the dealer could not make the prior verification, we were told to "just come back tomorrow," etc. Well, as we drove home, I was a bit frustrated to put it mildly. Yet, we came to see that God's hand of providence was involved all along. We did not get that vehicle. Instead, we found a wheelchair accessible van at a much lower cost, right here in Hudsonville across the street from the fairgrounds!

How has God's providence been seen in your life? Do you continue to thank Him for knowing and providing what we need, before we know what we really need?

Third, we should thank God for *sanctifying trials* (James 1:2-4; 1 Thes 5:18). When Corrie ten Boom's sister, Betsie, was giving thanks for fleas in their concentration camp bunkhouse at Ravensbruck, Corrie thought Betsie was crazy. Betsie replied, "We are to give thanks in all circumstances (1 The 5:18), including fleas." Later they found out that the fleas kept the guards away, which enabled the ten Booms to lead Bible studies and pray with the other women. The fleas and Betsie's prayer of thanks also showed Corrie the depths of her sinful heart. Ultimately, Corrie was able to give thanks amidst sanctifying trials.

I encourage you in the month of November to ask God to cultivate a thankful heart in you. Record the things for which you are thankful. Express your thanks to God. Never let Him hear the end of your thankful heart. Then share those things with your church family.

"Lord, you have given me so much. Give me one thing more. A grateful heart."

Oh, My Aching Back

December 2011

The answers are:

1) Bulging disk
2) Six times
3) Yes, a few years ago
4) I know. She is amazing
5) Pray for me

You will have to wait for the questions at the end.

Let me share a couple of things I learned while looking up at the ceiling for nearly two weeks. Pain is not something we readily sign up for, but it actually is a good teacher, making us aware of things we otherwise would miss or ignore.

First, I was reminded of the truth of 1 Corinthians 12:25-26. *"But God has so composed the body, giving greater honor to the part that lacked it, that there may be no division in the body, but that the members may have the same care for one another. If one member suffers, all suffer together; if one member is honored, all rejoice together."*

We all tend to take those little vertebrae for granted. Who really gives them a second thought? But once we make a few trips to the chiropractor's office and read those posters on the wall, we are amazed at the important functions those vertebrae do. Especially C-1 to S-5, not to mention L-2.

The same is true spiritually, regarding the Lord's church. Every person you meet at church who is a child of God is an important member of His body. We ought not to elevate people with certain gifts over those who have a different gift. Just as God knew what He was doing when he made our human body with a combination of thirty vertebrae (eight cervical, twelve thoracic, five lumbar and five sacral), He knows what He is doing when He places people in a church body with various spiritual gifts and functions.

To all those who serve behind the scenes with gifts of mercy and hospitality and kindness. . . thank you. To those who use gifts of administration and planning to ensure things are done properly and in order. . . thank you. To those who give quietly and generously with their gifts of giving. . .thank you. To those who come along side and give counsel and exhortation to those who are wandering or confused. . .thank you. To those who delight to pray and bring the church body before our heavenly Father. . . thank you. To those with a burden for those who are spiritually lost. . . Thank you. To those who love to help others. . . Thank you.

I hope you have found a place of service within the church God has placed you, and you are using the gifts God has given you for the benefit of others. If not, the body suffers and is not functioning properly.

Let me encourage you to express thanks to others in the body for their service. Find someone who is different from you, observe how God has made them and how God is using them, and then let them know that you appreciate their service for others.

Second, I was reminded of 2 Corinthians 1:3-6. "Blessed be the God and Father of our Lord Jesus Christ, the Father of mercies and God of all comfort,who comforts us in all our affliction, so that we may be able to comfort those who are in any affliction, with the comfort with which we ourselves are comforted by God. For as we share abundantly in Christ's sufferings, so through Christ we share abundantly in comfort too. If we are afflicted, it is for your comfort and salvation; and if we are comforted, it is for your comfort, which you experience when you patiently endure the same sufferings that we suffer. Our hope for you is unshaken, for we know that as you share in our sufferings."

There is something about pain which sensitizes us to the pain of others. When you have had back problems, you truly empathize with others. When you know the pain of disappointment, a miscarriage or a wayward child, the pain of marital discord, financial strain, or the struggle with depression, it makes you sensitive to the hurts of others.

What pain has God allowed in your life? Has it sensitized you to the hurts of others? Have you experienced God's comfort through His Word? What have you learned? Are you sharing that comfort with others? Who do you know in the body that is going through a season of pain with which you are familiar? How can you reach out to them with compassion and care?

Finally, let us know that God calls Himself, "the father of all mercies and God of all comfort." Isn't that good? May you know His mercies and comfort amidst your trials and pain.

Now for the questions:

1. What happened to your back?
2. Have you gone to a chiropractor?
3. Has this happened before?
4. Lois must be working hard to take great care of you. (Yes, I know this is not a question. But everyone says it.)
5. Is there anything we can do to help?

"I Do" - Then Doing It

March 2012

One of the privileges of being a pastor is that you have the best seat in the house when it comes to watching couples exchange their wedding vows. In fact, it is even better than the best seat, as I stand close enough to catch every nuance as the husband-to-be and the bride-to-be look each other in the eye and "repeat after me." Misty eyes and quivering lips all communicate that this is a sacred moment, the deepest promise one human being can make to another.

In my premarital counseling with couples, I think it is important to go over the vows they will exchange, before God and before witnesses. We discuss almost every phrase in this holy covenant. Here are the words that we discuss (the bride's words are nearly the same, with one significant exception.)

"Do you have this woman to be your wife; to live together in the holy covenant of marriage? Do you promise to love her, comfort her, honor and keep her, in sickness and in health, and forsaking all others, be faithful to her so long as you both shall live? If so, answer, 'I do.'"

The words above are called the "Declaration of Consent," an

affirmative answer given to the pastor indicating that a person is entering into this covenant of his or her own free will, without coercion. Then follows the "Vow Proper."

"I, _____, take you, _____, to be *my wife, to have and to hold, from this day forward, for better for worse, for richer for poorer, in sickness and in health, to love and to cherish, until death do us part; as God is my witness, I give you my promise.*"

Several times throughout the year, in preparation for upcoming weddings, I sit down with a couple and discuss these vows for almost an hour. As we do this, I often find myself thinking, "I hope this is helpful to the couple, but I know it is helpful to me." How so? It is good to think over what I vowed to do nearly thirty-one years ago.

Am I loving my wife? Comforting her? Honoring her? Keeping her? Er. . .what does *that* mean? I don't want to give away too many answers to prospective couples-to-be, but "keep" means "to provide for and take care of."

How about forsaking all others? Being faithful? Cherishing? What about the qualifying phrases: in sickness and in health? For better and for worse? For richer and for poorer? Until death do us part? That about covers the waterfront doesn't it? No loopholes. No exceptions. Nothing can arise that will render the covenant null and void. Cancer? Loss of a job? Old age?

I don't have any statistical proof to back this up, but my suspicion is that many of us "old-timers" in marriage aren't going to as many weddings as we used to. It used to be that almost everybody would show up for a "church wedding." You look around and it would almost seem like a Sunday morning worship service. Everyone was there. About twenty years ago, it seems to me, things began to change. My hunch is that when full-dinner receptions began to be the norm, it limited the number of invitations to a wedding. As a result, people don't attend as many weddings as they used to.

Maybe you are thinking? "What's wrong with that? It gives me more time to do my yard work!" Well, I am all for nice looking lawns, but I think we also lose something when we don't take time to hear and reflect on wedding vows, asking ourselves afresh how we are doing at keeping our vows. Frankly, it is good for us to listen to a young couple exchange their vows with misty eyes and quivering lips. It is a good reminder how important this holy covenant of marriage truly is.

So, take a moment and review the vows. In the rough and tumble of life, have you grown a bit hardened or passive toward your marriage? Have the many responsibilities of life and family taken a toll on you and your spouse? Are things dull and routine?

Let me encourage you to pick out one phrase from the vows that stands out the most to yo? Which phrase is it? Why does it seem highlighted? What does it mean to you? What does that part of the vows look like in your marriage? What do you need to do differently to fulfill better that portion of your vow?

Our whole relationship with God, and our whole eternity, is based upon God keeping His vows and promises to us. In return, may He find us faithful to the vows we make before Him and one another.

"For you, O God, have heard my vows; you have given me the heritage of those who fear your name. So will I ever sing praises to your name, as I perform my vows day after day" (Psalm 61:5,8).

"Sleep Well, My Friend"

"That's the last wire I need to attach to your skull. Have a good night and sleep well, Mr. Krogh." With those words, Curt, the nice technician at the Sleep Disorder Clinic, turned out the nice lights and shut the nice door. I laid on the nice bed, with my head on the nice pillow, knowing that nice Curt was watching me via a microphone, monitoring my every movement, including my breathing lungs, beating heart, twitching eye and soon-to-be-snoring nose.

Before he shut the door he reassured me, "You need to have twenty 'sleep events' (i.e. abnormalities) in the next two hours in order for you to get a passing score on the sleep study. You will know that you passed if I come wake you up in the middle of the night and put a mask over your face."

Well, aren't those cheery thoughts? I have always done well in school, but how exactly do you *pass* this test, when you are supposed to be unconscious? Let's see. First, I need to sleep. Not that easy with twenty wires hanging from your head, face, index finger, chest, legs. Second, I only get one pillow, not two. Third, I have to sleep on my back, not my side or stomach. Fourth, it's hot in here. Fifth, I can hear people talking in the hallway. Sixth, why isn't my wife sleeping next to me? Oh, that's right, she was the one who got me committed to this institution in the first place. Something about my snoring keeping her awake. Well, wait till she hears the results of this study. Something like, "Mrs. Krogh, your husband doesn't snore. In fact, he never went to sleep!" Seventh, you get the drift.

So, how exactly do you get to sleep knowing that Curt can probably read your mind if you do go to sleep? What if I fail this test and my sleeping privileges are forever revoked? I prayed for each member of my family, prayed for those in our church who had physical needs, prayed for those with spiritual needs. I recited the Lord's Prayer (not too loud, lest Curt admonish me for not sleeping. Well, on second thought, maybe it would be good for Curt.) I recited some memory verses (including Proverbs 6:4. A fitting verse for this sleep center. Look it up.) I thought about riding my motorcycle through the U.P. I thought about our daughter Kate having a baby in March, which made me remember when Luke was born right here in this hospital. Which made me think of . . . .how I was not sleeping!

Next thing I knew, Curt was saying, "Congratulations. You passed. It's 12:30 a.m. Let me put this mask over your nose." I wasn't this relieved to pass a test since the final exam in second year Hebrew in seminary. Next thing I knew, the bodiless voice of Curt was intoning through the speaker, "Good morning, Steve. It's 5:30 and you can go home as soon as I disconnect the wires."

Sleep. Something we all take for granted. Sleep is mentioned in the Bible 129 times, slumber eleven times. Paul twice mentions "sleepless nights" (2 Cor. 6:5; 11:27), which had nothing to do with Curt and everything to do with being persecuted for the gospel.

King Solomon said sleep is "sweet" (Ecclesiastes 5:12). He also said God "gives to His beloved even in his sleep" (Psalm 127:2).

Imagine that! God gives and blesses His people whom He loves even as we sleep. Even while you were sleeping last night, God was ruling the world with a sovereign hand. His eyes were watching over His people, from dirt-floored huts in Cameroon to snow-covered homes in America's Midwest. While you were sleeping, God was alert, graciously giving to and blessing you.

Sleep. Something we need in order to survive. We are creatures. Weak. Fragile. Frail. Clay. Dependent.

Thank you, LORD, that You who needs no rest, graciously gives to us who do need rest. Thank you, LORD, that You are our keeper. Today, tonight and for all eternity.

Feeling Your Pain: A Son's Dislocated Shoulder

I was settling in at the movie theater in Alpine with Susie and others from church to watch a documentary film about international adoption, when I got a phone call—Jacob had dislocated his shoulder at church. As I hopped on my motorcycle and sped to the ER, my mind flooded with memories. "Dislocation" was a word I am very familiar with. Shoulder dislocation was my specialty.

I dislocated my left shoulder on several occasions playing basketball in high school. The first time was at Monte Vista High School in San Diego. When the gym got silent and cheerleaders looked on in horror and began to cry, I knew this wasn't good. I will spare you the details, but surgery wasn't pursued because I was one of the rare individuals that dislocated both anterior and posterior. This meant that the only surgical solution was a complete fusion, leaving me unable to lift my hand over my head. That was a skill I wanted to retain if at all possible.

A memorable dislocation occurred in college when I was spending

132 *Topography: A Pastor's Reflection on the Terrain Between Sundays*

the night in an inner-city Los Angeles housing project, in the home of some boys from the boys club ministry I was involved in. Each night their dad took the battery out of their car so it wouldn't get stolen. When I dislocated my shoulder at 2:00 a.m., it took awhile for the dad to hook the battery up. He got flustered and I was in extreme pain, trying to give him directions in Spanish to the UCLA Medical Center. Somehow we entered the freeway via an exit ramp and drove one mile into oncoming traffic before we got turned around. That was the beginning of a very long night.

Another dislocation occurred in the middle of an elder retreat in the snow-capped mountains of Northern California. It was a unique ambulance ride. Don't think they ever finished the retreat.

My final dislocation occurred about eighteen years ago in a men's basketball league. It was one of those special nights when every shot went in. At half time I had scored 29 of my team's 32 points. I have witnesses. That night ended in the ER. I think we won anyway.

All that to say, Jake, I feel your pain. If you, the reader, want to share your dislocation story with me, I will feel your pain (as long as it wasn't a separation or a subluxation . . .those don't compare and you will get little sympathy.)

As I was talking to Jake, I shared two Scriptures with him. I remember reading in high school with utter amazement that the Bible spoke in two passages about orthopedic dislocation. The first has to do with Christ. The second with me.

First, Jesus knows the pain of dislocation. Psalm 22 is a Messianic psalm of David, meaning that David was describing his experience, but also foreshadowing the experience of the coming Messiah. David wrote: *"My tongue sticks to my jaws; they have pierced my hands and feet; I can count all my bones; they divide my garments among them, and for my clothing they cast lots; my bones are out of joint."* What David spoke of poetically, Jesus experienced literally. In crucifixion, often shoulders were dislocated. I believe this likely happened to Jesus on the cross. What agony.

As great as the physical pain of dislocation via crucifixion was, the spiritual pain was even worse. Jesus bore the just judgment of our sin on the cross, enduring the dislocation of separation from His Father, so that our souls could be "set right" with God.

Second, God wants us to avoid the pain of dislocation. The Christian life is like a long distance Christ-focused race, requiring both endurance and obedience. *"Therefore, lift your drooping hands and strengthen your weak knees, and make straight paths for your feet so that what is lame may not be put out of joint but rather be healed" (Hebrews 12:12).*

How are you doing in your Christian race? Is God calling you to endurance? Do you need to hang in there? Keep going? Not give up on your marriage, your job, your family, your friends? Is God calling you to finish well? Lift your drooping hands and strengthen your weak knees.

Or maybe God is calling you to obedience. Is God calling you to choose a straight path, rather than the crooked path which others are taking? Perhaps in a business venture or dealings with an associate? Is God calling you to resist or flee a place of temptation? What straight path is God calling you to? Will you walk that path? As difficult as it may be, the pain of dislocation is even greater.

Jake, I hope you never know the pain of another dislocation. I hope I never do, as well. Let us be thankful for a Savior who suffered dislocation so our souls could be put right. Let us follow Him with endurance and obedience.

"You Want to Do What?"

June 2013

"Dad, when I am old enough to drive, I want to get a pick-up truck."

When I heard those words coming out of my young teenage daughter, my first thought was, *Susannah, you don't really want a pick-up truck. I never had a pick-up truck. None of your four older siblings ever had a pick-up truck. In fact, I don't recall any of them even using the words "pick-up truck" in a complete English sentence. How could you want a pick-up truck?*

Two days before her sixteenth birthday, Susie, with our blessing, bought a pick-up truck. Here is the story and a lesson I learned through this.

God provided a great job for Susannah some time back. One of those "memorial stone" stories. She saved her money, kind grandpas put in a little extra for her birthday and dad spotted a pick-up right there on 32nd street: a 1994 Ford Ranger. We got some insight over the phone from our used car friends. Dan, the father of a young man in the church who had the same year truck, came along to make sure we took the truck for a ride but didn't get taken for a ride. (If you know what I mean.)

When it came time to close the deal, Susie was excited about negotiating the best price. I was like, "Susie, you don't really mean you enjoy haggling, do you? How could you enjoy that? I don't like to do that. I would never make your mother do that." With a little pre-coaching from Dan, she hopped out after the test drive, looked the guy in the eye and said, "I think I will need to replace these tires this winter. Don't you agree?" He stammered a bit and said, "Well, I supposed you are right." Susie said, "Okay than, I have saved up this amount of money. What can we do to get close to that number?" The man took Susie's opening salvo in stride, but stood firm: it was well below blue book, in good working condition, no rust, it had only been for sale for a few days, if it didn't sell in a week or two he could lower the price, but it was firm now.

Susie didn't bat an eye. Well, maybe she looked at him pleadingly, with those big blue eyes. The other father piped up from the driveway, "You know it would be her *first* vehicle. Imagine the happiness you will have in bringing her happiness. You remember your first car don't you?" As everyone pawed the ground with their feet, feeling uncomfortable. . .well, I guess it was just me feeling uncomfortable, I was getting the vibe that Susie, Dan, and even Shawn the Owner of All Happiness were actually enjoying all the drama.

I said, "Okay, no deal. Let's get in the car and we can go. We can sleep on it." Dan, wanting to be a part of the history being made, came to the rescue. "What if they came up with (a bit more than Susie had offered) cash today? We all walk away happy."

History was made. Dan was happy. Shawn was happier. Susie was happiest. I was worn out.

So what is the lesson?

Lesson one. God was teaching me again that people are different and God likes it that way. Kids can actually grow up under the same roof with the same parents, speak the same language, eat the same food and one daughter will want to play classical music, and the other daughter will want to drive a pick-up truck and listen to country western. Go figure. Just because I don't enjoy negotiating over a twenty-year-old truck doesn't mean that Susie doesn't. Enjoy looking at life through God's eyes. Look at the extreme diversity in creation. Look at the variety of plants in your garden. Look at the variety of birds at your feeder. God enjoys making people unique and distinct. We should learn to enjoy what God apparently enjoys.

Lesson two. We need to listen carefully to what people are actually saying, not hearing them say what we think or want them to say. When Susie was saying, "Dad, I would like to drive a pick-up truck someday," I was thinking, "No you don't." When she dialed the radio to country western, I was thinking, "You can't actually like that. Those songs are about . . well. Er. . . pick-up trucks." Develop the skill of being a good listener. Listen to what people are really saying. Ask questions. Then listen.

Lesson three. Parents, stand firm on biblical issues and standards, but when it comes to things down the ladder of importance, listen to your kids and allow them to be different from you. Allow them to be different from their siblings. Allow them to be who God made them to be: individuals with their own distinct enjoyments and personalities. As you flex on secondary things, hopefully your kids will learn a greater respect for you on the primary things.

Well, that's all for now. I've gotta go teach Susie how to use that stick shift. Hope she can hear me over her music.

Tree of Shame

With a sigh of relief, the last of 318 curves disappeared in my rear view mirror. "The Dragon," an internationally famous eleven-mile stretch of road in the Tennessee Smoky Mountains had been conquered. My friends and I had made it through curves with ominous names: Copperhead Corner, Hog Pen Bend, Brake or Bust Bend, Sunset Corner, Gravity Cavity and Beginner's End. Sparks flew as my foot-boards scraped on the asphalt in a few of the sharpest curves, but both I and my motorcycle emerged unsecathed.

Others weren't so fortunate. The name speaks for itself. "The Tree of Shame." Prominently placed at the Tail of the Dragon, it is adorned with the various relics of motorcycle wrecks: fenders, seats, windshields, rims, shattered helmets, mangled metal, twisted chrome. Reminders that sometimes the Dragon wins.

As I stood gazing at the tree, these thoughts came to mind.

First, the Dragon wins by deceit. The Dragon, that ancient Serpent, who is called the devil and Satan, the deceiver of the whole world (Revelation 12:9; 20:2) is all about deceit. Deceit is the concealment or distortion of the truth for the purpose of misleading.

The Devil loves deceit. He loves what he can win by deceit. Jesus said of the Devil, *"He has nothing to do with the truth, because there is no truth in him. When he lies, he speaks out of his own character, for his is a liar and the father of lies" (John 8:44).*

He fools people with deceptive curves of money, sensuality, power, lust, self-love, invincibility, anger, dissipation. If all else fails, he resorts to the sharpest curve of all—pride.

Unsuspecting people may think- "My parents are so lame." "There is nothing wrong with this." "I can do this in secret; nobody will ever find out." "I deserve this." "This will make me happy." - not knowing whose rebellion is behind those thoughts. His diabolical goal is not mangled metal, but hell-bent souls. Unfortunately, he often wins, as *"the way is broad that leads to destruction and many are those who enter by it" (Matthew 7:13).*

What lie is the Devil feeding you? What deceitful curve does he want you to race through?

Second, many people glory in things they should be ashamed of. The people who nailed their motorcycle parts to that tree weren't really ashamed. Quite the opposite.They were not ashamed of their misadventure, but gloried in it. They were proud to brag, "See that busted mirror up there? It's mine!" Hence, the autographs and dates on the various misshapen parts. The "Tree of Shame" is really tongue-in-cheek. There is no shame.

The apostle Paul's words regarding the ancient Greek culture well describe our culture today: *"For many walk as enemies of the cross of Christ. Their end is destruction, their god is their belly, and they glory in their shame, with minds set on earthly things" (Philippians 3:18-19).*

Athletes who cheat. Coaches who violate rules. Husbands who walk out on their wives. Fathers who abandon their children.

Politicians who act above the laws they make for others. People who redefine words to create their own reality, calling good evil and evil good. They glory in their shame.

Third, don't envy the wrongdoer. It may seem like the people who glory in their shame are smiling and getting away with it, while followers of Christ get the short end of the stick in the fun department. But if you notice the yellow sign on the railing behind the Tree of Shame, it reads, "Caution, watch for Falling Parts from Tree of Shame."

Indeed watch out! The Tree of Shame has falling parts. Sin eventually catches up with a person. If you glory in your shame and make your belly your god long enough, the end is destruction. The pleasures of sin are but for a season. Things look good for a while, but the standing grain has no heads and ultimately it yields no flour. If you sow the wind, eventually you reap a whirlwind (Hosea 8:7). The one who boasts in his shame is not to be envied, but pitied.

My dizzied mind full, I walked away from the tourist Tree with greater love for the One who bore our shame on the Tree that truly matters. Nailed to that tree are not pieces of plastic and metal, but our real sin and shame: *"He forgave us all our trespasses, by cancelling the record of the debt that stood against us with its legal demands. This he set aside, nailing it to the cross. He disarmed the rulers and authorities and put them to open shame, by triumphing over them in him" (Colossians 3:13, 14).* In bearing our shame, Jesus shames the Dragon and his demons.

Reflections of a Childhood Home

I am sitting in my dad's home office using his computer. Forty-three years ago this was my bedroom. With at least six moves by the time I reached sixth grade (my dad was a career Navy officer) it was God's blessing to live in this house through middle school, high school and college. It is the house my parents live in today.

It was extremely hot when we moved to San Diego the summer of 1970. While my parents searched for a home, my brother, sister and I hung out at the KOA campground, sweltering. We hoped and hoped Dad would find a home with a swimming pool. The choice came down to two homes: the one on Melrose Street with a glorious, shimmering pool and the "fixer upper" on Glen Abbey Boulevard. Melrose was nicer than any home I had ever seen. Plush. Luxurious. Did I mention the glorious, shimmering pool? Glen Abbey had knee-high weeds in the back and the previous owners had a pet monkey. You could tell how high the monkey could reach by the height of the dirty line around all the rooms of the house. I am serious.

While we kids chanted, "Mel-rose, Mel-rose, Mel-rose" in the oven-baked aluminum trailer at the KOA, my dad returned with the news we most dreaded. We were going to buy the monkey house. "It is a great deal. We can make something out of this. You will be able to go to a good school. All it needs is some elbow grease. There are four bedrooms. Everyone will have their own room." All the things well-meaning dads say. All we heard was "No swimming pool." All we could think about was, "A good deal? Of course it is a good deal. There used to be a monkey living there! My own bedroom? Great. Do I have to share it with the monkey?"

Our attitude began to change when Denny, the man with white leather shoes and a leisure-suit (hey, it was the 70's) showed up and walked our whole family into the weed-patch and said, "Right there is where it will go." Fortunately, he was selling Blue Haven pools, not monkey cages. Sure enough, in October a rumbling Caterpillar tractor was shaking the house as it tore through the fence and began scooping dirt. My mom was very nervous out as twenty laborers began spraying gunite on the rebar. She had few nerves left when the raised wall collapsed and everyone started yelling in Spanish. My dad was overseas doing what Navy men do to serve their country, so my mom and I (age 12) started to make executive decisions before the cement hardened. "Uh, Mom, I think that man is asking if we have a shovel."

My dad did return.The pool did get finished. My brother, sister and I jumped in. . . .even though it was October and the water was murky with plaster dust. For many months, even years, after a full day of work, my dad came home and set up portable lights to work at night, laying a flagstone patio around the pool that is a work of art to this day. The raised wall on one side of the pool would provide hours of fun as we stationed a basketball hoop up there and played "anything goes" water basketball.

So, as I look out the window of my monkey cage, er, old bedroom, at the shimmering pool, lots of memories flood my mind. I used to shoot hoops by the hour on that driveway. I used to throw a tennis ball on that roof. My brother and I used to run down that hall and jump over the pillows we stacked on the sofa when my mom wasn't home. Those are the sprinklers I helped my dad put in. Here are some life lessons.

1. Dads, if making a wise decision for what is right in the long-term means disappointing your kids in the short-term, do what is right. Disappoint the kids in the aluminum trailer. They will survive. Don't let their immature chants of "Melrose" make you do something you know isn't right. Choose the monkey house if it's the right thing to do.

2. Young people: Beware the tyranny of immediate gratification. Don't believe the lie that you can't be happy unless you have the latest and greatest gadget right now. The peaches that taste the sweetest come from the trees you planted and cared for. If your parents do give you the monkey business, remember they still love you. And they actually know more than you do. Hard to believe, but true.

3. Young marrieds: "Better is a little where love is than a fatted ox and strife with it."

4. All of us: Sanctification is more like Glen Abbey Boulevard than Melrose Street. The weeds of remaining sin need to be pulled up. The dirt of the monkey business of sin needs to be scrubbed off. Take a long-term view. Keep at the Christian life. Keep following Jesus.

5. Me: Remember that "The lines have fallen to me in pleasant places; I have a beautiful heritage" (Psalm 16:6). Thanks, Dad and Mom, for all you have done for me, Dave and Connie. We are blessed. Thanks for choosing the monkey house, thanks for the elbow grease and thanks for great memories.

Now for a dip in that pool. Ahhhh.

The Tree Line

I was pretty much a city boy, and growing up in a military officer's home, I lived in places such as Whidbey Island, Norfolk, Alameda and San Diego. But now, as a new seminary grad, my wife, Lois, and I were in our first church, and I was becoming acquainted with things like pheasant hunting, calf pulling and almond harvesting. To tell you the truth, at the time, I couldn't tell a pistachio orchard from a walnut orchard from a prune orchard from an almond orchard.

But all that was about to change and, as it did, I learned something very important about the Christian life.

Every time I hurtled down orchard-lined Highway 32 between Orland and Chico in Northern California, I noticed a curious brown line on each tree trunk and would wonder why the trees had those dark lines. The best answer I came up with was that there must have been a flood here at one time and it discolored the bark on the lower part of the trees. Wrong.

When I shared my hypothesis with a rancher friend of mine, he laughed out loud and called out to his wife, "Margie, come hear what

144   *Topography: A Pastor's Reflection on the Terrain Between Sundays*

our pastor just said." I knew I was about to get a lesson in Agriculture 101. I did.

That mysterious "line" was really the demarcation between two different types of walnuts grafted together to make one tree. The Paradox walnut is used for the root stock, as it has the best root system for absorbing water and nutrients from the soil. The Chandler walnut is used for the scion, the shoot grafted into the root stock when the tree is still young, as it is superior for bearing nuts on its branches.

Clever these ranchers are, getting the best of all possible worlds.

One day I knelt in the dirt on a cherry orchard and watched an arborist carefully grafting some trees. He made a slit in the root stock with the sharp blade of his knife, cutting at an angle through the outer bark into the heart of the young tree. Then with a flick of his wrist he made a similar cut in the scion. He carefully joined the two exposed flaps of the root-stock and scion, added some gluey pitch and wrapped them in tape. It was all done in less than one minute. On to the next tree.

"That will never work," I muttered to myself. "Two pieces of wood held together by glue and tape?" But it did. A few years later, I stood in that same orchard as my friend Bob watched truckloads of his cherries head down Interstate 5 to the Stockton shipyards. Those cherries, the first to ripen in the United States, fetched an amazing price when they landed in Japan within 24 hours.

Grafting: "a horticultural technique whereby tissues of plants are joined so as to continue their growth together." Defined by Wikipedia. Invented by God. Used by ranchers worldwide.

Three lessons. First, **security**. If you are a Christian, God has grafted you into Jesus Christ. Through the miracle of repentance and faith, a small slit was cut into your soul and you were joined to

Jesus in a living union. His life is now in us. We are "hidden with Christ in God," (Colossians 3:3) "joined to the Lord" so that we are "one spirit with him." (1 Corinthians 6:17) Because we are "in Christ" (the Apostle Paul's favorite description for believers), "neither death nor life, nor angels nor rulers, nor things present nor things to come, nor powers, nor height nor depth, nor anything else in all creation, will be able to separate us from the love of God in Christ Jesus our Lord." (Romans 8:38, 39) We are secure, knowing that in the right hands, grafting works.

Second, **expectancy**. Farmers expect their grafted trees to produce fruit. So should we. "If you abide in me, and my words abide in you, ask whatever you wish, and it will be done for you. By this my Father is glorified, that you bear much fruit and so prove to be my disciples. As the Father has loved me, so I have loved you. Abide in my love." (John 15:7-9) We are expectant, knowing that as we live in trusting, loving dependence on Jesus, we will bear fruit.

Third, **humility**. God in his mercy has joined us, Gentiles, into the rootstock of his covenant promises to Abraham. That should keep all of us humble. "But if some of the branches were broken off, and you, although a wild olive shoot, were grafted in among the others and now share in the nourishing root of the olive tree, do not be arrogant toward the branches. If you are, remember it is not you who support the root, but the root that supports you. . . .They were broken off because of their unbelief, but you stand fast through faith. So do not become proud, but fear" (Romans 11:17, 18, 20). We are humble, recognizing that God in his mercy has included us in something way beyond what we deserve.

A few weeks ago, I returned to visit friends in Northern California. Traveling down Highway 32 brought back many memories. But when I drove past that old familiar walnut orchard and saw the familiar lines on the trees, I wasn't wondering if an imaginary flood had made the lines.

Instead, I prayed, "Thank you, Father, for grafting me into your Son"—my heart filled with security, expectancy and humility.

On this your 60th Birthday . . .

What a pleasure to write for Steve on the occasion of his 60th birthday!

This date is a milestone for all of us and marks the transition to - *almost* old age. Steve, I remember well when we first became acquainted. I was the founding pastor of Brea Olinda Friends Church, and you and Lois were students at Biola. So, you heard me when I had just begun my preaching and exercising my new pastoral persona. Those were exciting days in sun, Southern California. I remember then that you were theologically astute and, happily, opinionated - and looking forward to going to Dallas Seminary.

We didn't see much of one another while you were at DTS, but your good friend and my brother-in-law, Wil Triggs, kept me apprised of "what was going with the Kroghs." Following Dallas, there came your lengthy pastorate in the Sacramento Valley. We connected periodically and talked pastoralia when Barabara and I were at College Church in Wheaton. Do you remember the tête-à-têtes that Barbara and I and you and Lois had about ministry, and what God has called us to? We certainly remember them with a smile.

During your years in Hudsonville, you did me the great honor of inviting me to speak to some pastors in your area and then occupy your pulpit. So, I got to see you *in situ*. That's when I came to appreciate you even more. You have been a great example to me of godly integrity and commitment to biblical principle. All this, and this does not indicate how much fun you and Lois are. Barbara and I cherish you both.

Of course, after we left Wheaton, you came to Wheaton! That's not fair, because we're now 2,000 miles away. I want you to know that as you continue your ministry with *Training Leaders International*, that we regularly pray for you and Lois.

As you grow older, the years will fly by like fence posts on an Illinois country road, but the beautiful thing is, we're headed towards the sunrise. Steve, thanks for your friendship and example over the years.

Dominus vobiscum,

Kent Hughes
Westminster Theological Seminary

Steve and I met many years ago in Hudsonville because I had been asked to speak to the FIRE Conference held in the church he pastored at the time. We immediately became friends, which was strengthened by years of contact on the FIRE board and at gatherings, plus several trips to Hudsonville where I got to know your wonderful family and walked and talked in the woods. We went to Brazil together, adding to our bond.

Steve, I count you as a genuine friend and servant of Christ. You've handled life in front my eyes in such a noble way, caring deeply to love Christ above all. Thanks for these years of great memories and encouragement from your words and ministry. The best is ahead.

Jim Elliff
Christian Communicators Worldwide

I've had the personal joy of walking with Steve for decades and this has given me a growing sense of gratitude for his tender love and godly character. From our first meeting in Orland to the present I've admired his constancy in being a humble servant without the need to be first. He counts others better than himself and he has sought first Christ's kingdom in the process.

He has been a model teacher of the Word and willing to do right regardless of the circumstances. He gave much to support and advance me in my ministry and I remain deeply grateful and have the most profound respect for him.

Well done good and faithful brother.

John H. Armstrong
Act3 Network

I had the privilege of serving alongside Steve for 15 years. I was grateful for his wisdom, his wry sense of humor, and his leadership. Anyone who has spent any time with Steve can attest to the wisdom that he possesses by his dwelling in the Word of God. Not only that, but he also has the gift of capturing and presenting his thoughts in such a pithy and compelling way through his pen! The writings contained in this book will inspire, motivate, encourage, and challenge you to also drink deeply of the Word of God and to serve Him faithfully wherever God has planted you.

Brian Felten
Worship Pastor, Grace Community Church, Hudsonville

I met Steve Krogh, a recent Seminary graduate, when he arrived at the Orland Evangelical Free Church in 1985. I knew right off the bat he was a good fit when he joined the Cleek family Sunday lunch and traditional whiffle ball game as the most vigorous player who chased a fly ball through the zinnias and the wood fence to come up with the out.

Steve, David Sotelo, and I met weekly for prayer on Tuesday nights from around 10 pm until around 2 or 3 am. It was a unifying time of camaraderie as we sought the Lord together. The ideas for Real People Camp for 3rd-6th graders and Cowboy Sunday were birthed from those nights of prayer. God used Steve's gift for organization to bring these ideas to fruition. We also prayed for people to come to the Lord. One year we saw God answer our prayers mightily as 100 people prayed to receive Christ. Steve was not only a man of prayer but also a man of action. I was privileged to serve as an elder with these two pastors. One day Steve informed me they were paid to be good and I was good for nothing. Needless to say he has a good sense of humor.

It was no surprise to see Steve's teaching skills grow rapidly in his transition from student to pastor. His biblical knowledge and insights were exceptional. With his special gift for teaching and love for God's Word, Steve became and outstanding expositor. I also have to say I never laughed so hard during a sermon as I did when Steve related "the hunting trip story". I had tears running down my face and I was laughing so hard I couldn't breath.

Steve was gifted at creatively meeting people where they were in life. He traveled with one church member on his overnight tractor trailer haul. He washed a widow's dirty windows. He and Lois prepared a romantic dinner on the creek for a couple's wedding anniversary. He built a life sized Goliath figure, which he placed at the creek for a group of adventurous boys to fight. Steve understood touching people's hearts for Jesus.

During 2003 – 2007 when I served in Cameroon, Steve twice brought a mission team to work on our field. While there, Steve taught in the seminary, did a baptismal service, and went with the team to the remote villages to show the Jesus Film. He had a special gift for ministering to the international church. The pastors and seminary students all loved him. God was preparing him, even then, for his current ministry.

In 2014 Steve became the campaign manage and consultant for Cleek for Congress. What exceptional vision and insight Steve had for a political campaign! I can only say our campaign suffered when we agreed it was time for us to move to a "professional" campaign manager.

Steve, we have had some great adventures. I look forward to the next thing God has for us to tackle together. You are a great man and a good friend. I thank God upon every remembrance of you.

Happy 60th birthday

Norris Eugene (Pokey) Cleek, MD

Orland, California

Happy birthday! Thanks for being a constant source of encouragement to me through the years. Your open and honest walk with the Lord is so refreshing. I'm quite sure you've not even realized that your love for God, your wife, children, and ministry have caused me to want to keep fighting the good fight. Your commitment to walk these days on earth with the end in mind is a real gift, and I'm so glad you've shared that with me. Not many men are blessed and have the privilege of seeing God's good hand extended to them in such visible ways in this life.

Thanks for pursuing the God of Heaven and sharing your love for Him with me. Thanks for being transparent, "real", and encouraging. Thanks for being such a good friend. Let's finish the race running as hard as we can.

Jeff Wolff
West Unit Principal, Centerville High School

I personally found Pastor Steve to be a great man of God, a humble man of integrity, kind and gentle. He has been a great help both at the College and to our Church. We dedicated our fourth son to the Lord bearing the name of Steve to honor him. We fondly remember Steve's family everyday.

Pastor Christoher John
Tarime, Tanzania

It may be hard to imagine, but there was a time when Steve Krogh did not know Greek, had never preached a sermon, not travelled overseas or even met Lois. Thrown into the freshman class at Biola, we were roommates for a few hours, and then had our room assignments changed. By choice, we were again roommates for much of our time as undergrads. So what do I remember about Steve from all those years ago?

Looking back, I see seeds of the man he would become. A quiet kindness. A good sense of humor. A dawning interest in missions. Basketball. A heart that cared for others. It seems that as we scrambled through Bible and theology classes, we both stood at the base of the Everest of God's Word that even still we are barely starting to climb. I am so grateful that God had allowed us some shared vistas of grace over all these years. Now, to come together at College Church and in our small group, such a provision of God's goodness and handiwork in our lives!

Wil Triggs
Director of Communications
College Church of Wheaton

What I love most about Steve is his intentional encouragement. He's one of the few people in my life that will on occasion write me a note telling me he appreciates how I've done something or that I'm going in the right way or to keep going. I know Steve is a talented teacher and pastor, but he excels even more as a great encourager. He has wise words at right moments for people who need them. It is just one of the reasons I feel privileged to work with him.

Darren Carlson
President, Training Leaders International
Minneapolis, Minnesota

155

About the Author

Steve Krogh (B.A., Bible and Humanities, Biola University, 1980; Th.M., Old Testament, Dallas Theological Seminary, 1985) pastored for thirteen years at the Evangelical Free Church in Orland, California and for fifteen years at Grace Community Church in Hudsonville, Michigan. Since 2014 he has been involved in theological training for pastors around the world, serving with Training Leaders International in a variety of countries, including Serbia, Mongolia,Tanzania, Malawi, India, Liberia, Brazil, Togo and Ethiopia.

Steve has been married to Lois for 38 years. They have six children—two now married—and four grandsons. They live in West Chicago, Illinois.

Steve climbs mountains, rides a Harley, builds great sandboxes and sells books through Northampton Books, his on-line bookstore.